T0291328

Gen Z Around the World

Gen Z Around the World: Understanding the Global Cohort Culture of Generation Z

EDITED BY

COREY SEEMILLER

Wright State University, USA

AND

MEGHAN GRACE

Plaid, LLC, USA

United Kingdom – North America – Japan – India – Malaysia – China

Emerald Publishing Limited
Emerald Publishing, Floor 5, Northspring, 21-23 Wellington Street, Leeds LS1 4DL

First edition 2024

Reprints and permissions service
Contact: www.copyright.com

British Library Cataloguing in Publication Data
A catalogue record for this book is available from the British Library

ISBN: 978-1-83797-093-3 (Print)
ISBN: 978-1-83797-092-6 (Online)
ISBN: 978-1-83797-094-0 (Epub)

Printed and bound by CPI Group (UK) Ltd, Croydon, CR0 4YY

INVESTOR IN PEOPLE

Contents

List of Tables

About the Editors

Dr Corey Seemiller is a Professor in the Department of Leadership Studies in Education and Organizations at Wright State University. She is the author of *The Student Leadership Competencies Guidebook*, a prominent resource for developing youth and college student leadership programs. Her other books focus on today's young people and include *Generation Z Goes to College, Generation Z Leads, Generation Z: A Century in Making,* and *Generation Z Learns.* Dr Seemiller's work has been featured on NPR and in *The New York Times, Time Magazine, Newsweek,* as well as in several other news publications and academic journals. She has also been interviewed for podcasts as well as TV and radio shows worldwide and has engaged in market research consulting for Fortune 10, 50, and 500 companies. Her highly popular *TED Talk* on Generation Z at TEDxDayton showcased how Generation Z is making a difference in the world.

Dr Meghan Grace is a Senior Consultant with Plaid, LLC, overseeing the firm's operations and strategy. She also leads the firm's research and assessment initiatives. Dr Grace is the coauthor of the books *Generation Z Goes to College, Generation Z Leads, Generation Z: A Century in Making,* and *Generation Z Learns.* She is the co-lead of the Institute for Generational Research and Education, a nonprofit with the mission to foster understanding, appreciation, and collaboration between generations. Dr Grace hosts the podcast #GenZ, where she shares the lived experiences and stories of members of Generation Z.

About the Contributors

Muhamad Irfan Agia is an Economic and Consumer Psychology practitioner who applies insights from psychology and behavioral economy to better understand consumer behavior, decision-making, and drive behavior change. With a Masters in Economic and Consumer Psychology from Leiden University and more than 6 years of experience in consumer and market research field, he helps businesses in the various industries from FMCG, Media, E-Commerce, Fintech, Investment, and F&B to empathize with their consumer and design frictionless journey experience.

Marta Hernández Arriaza is a Junior Researcher at Comillas Pontifical University in Madrid. She studied psychology and is certified as a therapist and vocational counselor. She is currently pursuing her PhD on the university experience of Generation Z.

Gonzalo Aza-Blanc is an Associate Professor of the Department of Psychology at the Pontifical Comillas University, Madrid, Spain. He teaches Cultural and Community Psychology and work as a Family Psychotherapist at Clinical Unit of Psychology (Uninpsi). He also conducts research as a member of the University's Polaris Project, with the goal of better understanding university students, how they transform themselves during their time at the university and how they project themselves into the future.

Francesca Beretta is an Assistant Teaching Professor and the Italian Language Program Director at the University of Kansas. Her main interests include pedagogy, instructional design, and inclusive practices for students with learning disabilities. She holds a PhD in Italian Stuwaechterdies from the University of Texas at Austin and an MA in Language and Linguistics from Lancaster University.

Diana Bogueva is a Social Scientist with interests in sustainable food consumption, alternative proteins, consumer perception of novel food processing technologies, generational consumer behavior, food sustainability and harmonization. Dr Bogueva's work has won several prestigious awards, including at the 24th and 28th Gourmand Awards, considered equivalent to the Oscars in the area of food books. Five of her refereed papers are scored in the top 5% in the world by Altmetric for the media attention they have received. Dr Bogueva has more than 40 refereed publications. She has been employed at the University of Sydney and is currently a Research Fellow at Curtin University where she also teaches in the unit People and Planet. Dr Bogueva has supervised two PhD students to successful completion. She is a Board Member, Working Groups Director, and Chair of the Consumer Perceptions Working Group of the international Global Harmonization Initiative headquartered in Vienna.

Elena Botezat is a Professor in the Department of Management-Marketing at the University of Oradea. Her academic research focuses in the last years on Generation Z's potential as future entrepreneurs and employees. Dr Botezat's more specific contributions relate to entrepreneurial intentions and Generation Z Workplace expectations. The research work followed a natural gradual process that sought to capitalize on the knowledge, skills, expertise, and opportunities from the documentation and specialization attained through teaching and research internships followed by scientific events participation and involvement in research–development projects with European funding. In line with a fast-growing interest, she has also designed and delivered didactic materials in such a way that they suit Generation Z members' demands.

Daniela Crișan is a Senior Data Scientist and Machine Learning Engineer active within a tech company in the North-West of Romania. Dr Crișan obtained her PhD in Psychometrics and Statistics at the University of Groningen, the Netherlands, in 2020. Her main interests are statistical modeling, data science, machine learning, artificial neural networks, natural language processing, and anomaly detection. Other interests include cognitive and noncognitive test/scale construction and validation, psychometric models, and research methodologies in the social and behavioral sciences.

Niva Dolev is a Senior Lecturer at the Education and Community department at Kinneret College on the Sea of Galilee, Israel. Her main research field is emotional intelligence, social-emotional competence (SEC), and positive psychology in organizations and in particular in education. Dr Dolev is the Dean of Students, a founding member of the Center of Applied Ethics and a member of the European Network for Social Emotional Competence (ENSEC). She is involved in interventions to prepare organizations and education systems for the 21st century and has led a number of social-emotional development educational initiatives for the ministry of education as well as social-emotional learning (SEL) school interventions and educators' trainings. She has also been interviewed for podcasts as well as TV and radio shows, and publishes newspaper articles on education and parenting.

Silvia Fotea is a Lecturer at the Emanuel University of Oradea, Griffiths School of Management and IT, Romania. Her research interests and efforts are directed toward understanding and solving challenges of managing and marketing the family business, understanding the attitudes and behaviors of young people (Gen Z), and the impact of technology on businesses, employees, and education. She is the author or coauthor of 3 books and 17 scientific articles.

Ioan Fotea is an Associate Professor at the Griffiths School of Management and IT within the Emanuel University of Oradea, Romania, where he serves as the Dean. His specific interests are in research methods and techniques for the economic and business phenomenon, especially in relationship marketing, technological advancements, and generational shifts.

Ronalyn I. Garcia is a Graduate of Bachelor of Science in Economics from Cavite State University. She is currently on her last phase toward completing her Master's degree in Business Administration at the same university. She has also earned units in Master of Arts in Economics at Polytechnic University of the Philippines. Ms Garcia serves as a statistician for most of the Gen Zers and that of the undergraduate and graduate students as well as a resource speaker on technical writing, data presentation, and infographics in various institutions and recently at the Philippine Statistics Authority.

Zahrotur Rusyda Hinduan or Rosie Hinduan is an Associate Professor with a long experience working in higher education management at the Faculty of Psychology Universitas Padjadjaran, Bandung, West Java, Indonesia. Her current research area is the development of digital-based psychological interventions for individuals from Generation Z. She has published a book chapter regarding Gen Z in Indonesia. Her other areas of research interest include the health psychology of young people, especially related to HIV/AIDS, Sexual Reproductive Health and Rights, and Drug Education as well as behaviors of young people at work. Her educational background in psychology is particularly useful when conducting behavioral change-related research. Her work has been published in respected journals such as Frontiers in Psychology and Asia Pacific Journal of Human Resource Management.

Stepanka Kadera is a Postdoctoral Scientist in the Department of Education and Rehabilitation at the Ludwig Maximilian University of Munich and in the Department of Family and Family Policy at the Deutsches Jugendinstitut e.V. in Munich. She is Membership Chair in the International Academy of Family Psychology (IAFP). Her research interests include family research, childhood and youth research, and capacity and quality building in child protection.

Mariya Karaivanova has been working as a Chief Assistant Professor in psychology at the Medical University of Plovdiv, Faculty of Public Health, Health Care Management Department in Bulgaria since 2018. She has defended a PhD thesis in Differential psychology studying generational differences in work preferences, perspectives about the future and life satisfaction at St. Kliment Ohridski University of Sofia, Bulgaria, in 2016. In the period 2016–2017 Mariya has made two postdoctoral research stays at the GESIS, Leibniz Institute for the Social Sciences in Cologne, Germany and at the Social Science Center in Berlin, Germany. Mariya coauthored a chapter on generation Z's characteristics, preferences and lifestyle in Bulgaria in the book *Generations Z in Europe: Inputs, Insights and Implications* published in 2019.

Dora Marinova is a Professor of Sustainability at Curtin University in Perth, Australia. Her work has been published in prestigious journals including Scientometrics, Journal of Cleaner Production, Journal of Econometrics and Nanotechnology. Professor Marinova is a leading expert on sustainability, the environmental impact of food (including meat consumption), and the newly emerging area of sustainometrics. With more than 380 refereed publications, she is one of the world's top authors in sustainability. She has also served on multiple panels of the Australian Medical and Health Research Council and supervised 75 PhD students to successful completion. She is nationally and internationally recognized as an Elected Fellow of two prestigious societies, including the Modeling and Simulation Society of Australia and New Zealand (MSSANZ) and International Environmental Modeling and Software Society (IEMSS) in Switzerland. Dora is also an Elected Member of the Australian Institute of Aboriginal and Torres Strait Islander Studies (AIATSIS).

Luisa M. Martinez is an Assistant Professor of Marketing and Research Coordinator at IPAM Lisboa, and Researcher at UNIDCOM/IADE in Lisboa, Portugal. She holds a PhD in Management, a Post-graduation in Management, a Master's in Color in Architecture, and a Degree in Architecture. Her research interests include the influence of color and sensitivity on organizational and consumer behavior. Topics such as retail, packaging, children marketing, digital marketing, well-being, and environment are considered. Her approach to research is interdisciplinary, as it incorporates diverse knowledge fields (e.g., management, marketing, psychology, education, design).

Radka Massaldjieva is a Professor of Clinical Psychology at Medical University of Plovdiv and teaches general, developmental, and applied psychology. She worked in the Psychiatric clinic of St. George University hospital in Plovdiv and during that time received a clinical qualification and diplomas of clinical psychologist and neuropsychologist from the Medical University in Sofia. She has a long experience in higher education and a practice of consultant and psychotherapist, and she is actively engaged in psychological counseling of students. She has led and participated in numerous research projects and has published scientific articles and book chapters in collaboration with researchers in neurology, psychiatry, and psychology.

Keba T. Modisane is a Scholar, Practitioner, and Educator. Currently, she is a Lecturer in Educational Leadership and Management. She is also the Founder of Basikwa Holdings – Women and Youth Entrepreneurship & Empowerment (PTY) Ltd and a Trustee of a Village Community Development Trust. Previously she was a human resources manager, a research manager, and high school teacher.

Liane Vina G. Ocampo is an Assistant Professor at Cavite State University. She completed her Bachelor of Science degree in Economics, went on to earn her Master's degree in Business Administration, and completed the academic requirements for PhD in Business Management. She has also held positions such as Campus Secretary for nearly three years and as Income Generating Project

Coordinator for more than two years. Her research findings have been showcased at numerous multidisciplinary conferences and enable her to publish econometrics and business research studies in esteemed journals.

Gudrun Quenzel is a Professor at the Institute for Sociology of Education at the University of Education in Vorarlberg (Austria). Her research focuses on youth, educational inequality, well-being, and the democratization of schools. She is author of the German "Shell Youth Survey," the Austrian Youth Survey "Lebenswelten 2020 - Values of young people in Austria," and coeditor of the journal "Discourse. Journal of Childhood and Adolescence Research" (Budrich). Recently, she published a book on student participation in schools in Germany, Austria, and Switzerland (Budrich).

Isabel Muñoz-San Roque is a Full Professor at the Universidad Pontificia Comillas de Madrid. She teaches subjects related to research methodology and statistics, as well as an educational innovation. She has a degree in Educational Sciences from the Complutense University of Madrid since 1994 and a PhD in Pedagogy from the Comillas Pontifical University since 2002. She is currently participating in two European projects (Addressing poor learning outcomes in primary education, Integration Mapping of Refugee and Migrant Children in Schools). In addition, she has coordinated several projects at the university on student cultures, higher education, key competencies in infant, primary and secondary education, and educational innovation.

Tamather Shatnawi is an Associate Professor at the University of Petra and the Head of the Marketing Department at the Faculty of Administrative and Financial Sciences. She has extensive marketing professional experience in the telecommunications sector, having worked for nearly 18 years at Jordan Telecom Group (Orange), one of France Telecom's affiliates, in areas such as marketing information systems, sales, and customer operations. Her research interests include digital marketing, new technology, and the marketing implications for future generations. She holds a Certified Digital Marketing Professional (CDMP) certification from Digital Marketing Insinuate (DMI).

Shefaly Shorey is an Associate Professor at Alice Lee Centre for Nursing Studies, Yong Loo Lin School of Medicine, National University of Singapore. Her research focuses on enhancing family health by developing psychosocial interventions to support vulnerable populations and inform practice and policy. Shorey is an award-winning educator who has incorporated varied educational theories, virtual reality, and artificial intelligence in her teaching and she has received various awards at International and National platforms for her academic and research excellence. She represents Singapore for the Southeast and East Asian Nursing Education and Research Network (SEANERN) and the Global Working Group (GWG) on Salutogenesis. Shorey has published more than 190 papers in peer-reviewed international journals, written two books and more than 10 book chapters, and served on the editorial boards of various renowned journals. For her research work, she serves on the expert panel of ministries to inform care and practice for varied populations.

Alfe Solina serves as an Associate Professor V, Management Department Chairperson and Graduate School Learning Center Coordinator at Cavite State University – Imus Campus in the Philippines. Dr Solina also serves as one of the training facilitators for the official delegates of government educational institutions from Asia and the Pacific regions. She is part of a Professional Training on Personnel Development and Further Training in Enterprises, through the Philippine government and Federal Republic of Germany bilateral project with collaboration training at International Labor Organization (ILO) in Turin, Italy. Dr Solina also serves as a country representative in the 2002 ASEAN Regional Training on Self-Employment for Out-of-School Youth in Hanoi, Vietnam together with the officials from the National Youth Commission, Office of the President of the Philippines. She has earned recognitions and awards in a number of occasions in the Best Paper (Professional) category, Best Abstract, Best Presenter, and as top finalist for Best Research Paper in different international conferences.

Eman Tarabia is a Researcher and Lecturer at Kinneret College on the Sea of Galilee and Western Galilee College. Her research focuses on social-emotional aspects among youth and higher education. She studied self-image, social competence, social-emotional support, effects, and correlations between different variables. She published articles in the field. During the Corona period, she led research on the subject of anxiety among Arab students in higher education and published an article. In 2022, she led a study on Hebrew language proficiency and its effect on self-image, motivation, and academic success among students, which was published in an article. Today she leads research on practical experience in academia and its effect on self-efficacy and a sense of optimism. Today, she officiates as the Head of the Education and Family Division in the Department of Multidisciplinary Studies and as the Director of the Hayatana Center for Shared Life at Kinneret College.

İsmail Hakkı Tekiner is an Assistant Professor in the Department of Nutrition and Food Engineering at Istanbul Sabahattin Zaim University, Istanbul, Türkiye. He received his BSE in chemical engineering from Middle East Technical University and completed his doctoral studies in Food Engineering at Istanbul Aydın University. His primary fields of interest are food safety and sustainability, food stability, nutrition, and space foods. He has more than 70 refereed publications, has supervised nine graduate-level students to successful completion, holds editorial and professional memberships roles in national and international journals and societies, and has conducted research on food sustainability and food stability funded by national (TÜBİTAK) and international (EU Horizon 2020) bodies. İsmail is also a member of the Global Harmonization Initiative (GHI). Since October 2022, he has been a guest academic and researcher in the Department of Industrial Biotechnology of Ansbach University of Applied Sciences, Ansbach, Germany.

Daria Vyugina is an Associate Professor at the Faculty of Journalism at Lomonosov State University and the Chair of Media Theory and Economics. She participated in two large-scale studies of Generation Z: firstly, as the author of Generation Z in Russia: The Digital Divide of the Generation Putin in the book *Generations Z in Europe-Inputs, Insights and Implications* (2019) and later as the coauthor of the book *Media Consumption of the Digital Youth in Russia* (2021).

Natalia Waechter is a Professor in the Department of Educational Science at the University of Graz. Her research focuses on generations, young people, digitalization, social inequalities, identity, migration, as well as comparative empirical studies. At the Ludwig-Maximilian University Munich, she is leading the team of the H-2020 project *ySKILLS* investigating digital skills of young people. Her most recent monograph is *The Construction of European Identity among Ethnic Minorities: "Euro-Minorities" in Generational Perspective* (Routledge). She is editorial board member of the *Austrian Journal of Sociology* (Springer), *Emerging Adulthood* (SAGE), and *Youth and Globalization* (Brill).

Acknowledgments

We would like to thank all of the educators, scholars, and practitioners from across the globe who made the research for this book possible. They include:

Australia

- Diana Bogueva, Centre Manager at Centre for Advanced Food Engineering (CAFE), The University of Sydney.
- Dora Marinova, Professor of Sustainability, Curtin University of Technology.

Austria

- Gudrun Quenzel, Professor at the Institute for Sociology and Education, University of Education of Vorarlberg.
- Natalia Waechter, Professor, Department of Educational Science, University of Graz.

Belgium

- Maarten Leyts, Youth Culture Expert and Marketeer, Community Builder, and Founder of Trendwolves.

Botswana

- Keba Modisane, Independent Scholar, Basikwa Holdings- Women & Youth Entrepreneurship & Empowerment (PTY) Ltd, Gaborone.

Brazil

- Gustavo Severo De Borba, Director of the Institute for Innovation in Education and Professor of Design at Unisinos.
- Isa Mara Rosa Alves.
- Paula Campagnolo, Professor in the Nutrition and Food Graduate Program and Academic Manager of Undergraduate Courses at Unisinos University.
- Sergio Eduardo Mariucci.
- Lara Maria Luft, Writer and Language Teacher.

- Debora Barauna, Professor at Unisinos Design School.
- Cristiane Schnack, Teaching Development Manager and Professor of the Literature Course, and of the Academic Activity of Personal and Professional Development.

Bulgaria

- Mariya Karaivanova, Chief Assistant Professor in Psychology, Department of Health Care Management, Faculty of Public Health, Medical University of Plovdiv, Bulgaria.
- Kristina Kilova, Chief Assistant Professor at Department of Medical Informatics, Biostatistics and e-Learning, Faculty of Public Health at Medical University of Plovdiv.
- Desislava Bakova, Associate Professor at Department of Health Care Management, Faculty of Public Health at Medical University of Plovdiv.
- Antonia Yaneva, Faculty of Public Health at Medical University of Plovdiv.
- Mariya Semerdzhieva, Faculty of Public Health at Medical University of Plovdiv.
- Radka Massaldjieva, Professor, Faculty of Public Health, Medical University of Plovdiv, Bulgaria.

China

- Lily Li, English Instructor in the School of Foreign Languages at Weifang Medical University.
- Jinlong Chen, Management Instructor in the School of Tourism Management at Leshan Normal University.
- Dongling Si, English Teacher in Leshan E-bridge Pre-school.
- Minghua Zhang, English Instructor in the School of Foreign Languages at Dongchang College Liaocheng University.

Cyprus

- Blend Ibrahim, Assistant Professor in the Department of Tourism Management, School of Tourism and Hospitality Management at Girne American University.

Ecuador

- Borja Guerrero-Bocanegra, Doctoral Researcher at UNED in the Education Program.

Germany

- Christine Hunner-Kreisel, former Professor of Transculturality and Gender at University of Vechta.
- Stepanka Kadera, Senior Lecturer for Pedagogic at the Ludwig Maximilian University of Munich.
- Katharina Rathmann, Professor, Fulda University of Applied Sciences.

Hong Kong

- Melanie Zhan, Part-Time Lecturer in the School of Communication at Hong Kong Baptist University.

India

- Shaheema Hameed, Curriculum Developer in Aspire Academy under the Aspire Zone Foundation in Doha, Qatar.
- Meera Mathur, Professor of Management Studies at Mohanlal Sukhadia University.
- Ashish Gupta, Assistant Professor at the Indian Institute of Foreign Trade, New Delhi, Ministry of Commerce and Industry, Government of India.

Indonesia

- Zahrotur Rusyda Hinduan, Faculty of Psychology Universitas Padjadjaran.
- Adilla Anggraeni, Deputy Head of Business Management and Marketing at Universitas Binus.
- Shafia Islaha, Faculty of Psychology at Universitas Padjadjaran.
- Irwan Pranoto, Professor in Biblical Studies and Practical Theology and Director of Younger Generation Ministry Research Center at Southeast Asia Bible Seminary.
- Muhamad Irfan Agia, PT, Bibit Tumbuh Bersama, Indonesia.

Israel

- Niva Dolev, Senior Lecturer at the Education and Community Department and Dean of Students, Kinneret College on the Sea of Galilee.
- Yael Livneh, Lecturer, Human Resource Management at Kinneret College on the Sea of Galilee.
- Eman Tarabia, Lecturer, Department of Multidisciplinary Studies, Kinneret College on the Sea of Galilee.

Italy

- Sebastiano Benasso, Senior Assistant Professor in the Department of Education Sciences at the Università degli Studi di Genova.
- Valentina Cuzzocrea, Associate Professor of Political and Social Sciences at the Università di Cagliari.
- Francesca Beretta, Assistant Teaching Professor, Italian Language Program Director, University of Kansas.

Jordan

- Tamather Shatnawi, Head of Marketing Department in the Faculty of Administrative & Financial Sciences at University of Petra.
- Abeer Alkhwaldi, Associate Professor and the Head of the Marketing Department at the Faculty of Administrative and Financial Sciences, University of Petra.

Lebanon

- Gloria Abdo, Director of Student Life and Senior Lecturer at Saint Joseph University of Beirut.

Montenegro

- Boban Melovic, Vice Dean for International Cooperation and Associate Professor in the Faculty of Economics at University of Montenegro.
- Milica Vukcevic, Teaching Assistant in the Faculty of Economics at University of Montenegro.

The Netherlands

- Aart Bontekoning, Social Psychologist, Consultant, and Speaker at Generatiewerk.
- Maarten Brand, Owner of Bureau Brand.
- Wijnand de Jong, Social Psychologist and Lecturer of Applied Sciences at University of Amsterdam.

Philippines

- Alfe M. Solina, Department of Management Chairperson and Graduate School Learning Center Coordinator, Cavite State University Imus Campus.
- Baby Kharen A Cristal, Instructor in the Department of Management at Cavite State University Imus Campus.
- Sixto N. Ras Jr., Department of Physical Education Chairperson, Cavite State University Imus Campus.

- Liane Vina G. Ocampo, Assistant Professor, Cavite State University Imus Campus.
- Ronalyn I. Garcia, Master in Business Administration Graduate Student, Cavite State University Imus Campus.

Portugal

- Luis Martinez, Associate Professor and Academic Co-Director of the Master's in Management at the Nova School of Business and Economics.
- Luisa M. Martinez, Assistant Professor of Marketing and Research Coordinator, IPAM.
- Luiza R. Haddad, PhD candidate in Marketing at Nova School of Business and Economics, Portugal.
- Filipe R. Ramos, Assistant Professor at the Faculty of Sciences, University of Lisbon, Portugal.

Romania

- Elena Aurelia Botezat, Professor, Department of Management and Marketing, Faculty of Economics, University of Oradea.
- Silvia Fotea, Assistant Professor at Griffiths School of Management and IT, Emanuel University of Oradea.
- Ioan Fotea, Associate Professor and Dean of The Griffiths School of Management and IT, Emanuel University of Oradea.
- Daniela Crişan, Data Scientist.

Russia

- Daria Vyugina, Associate Professor, Faculty of Journalism, Lomonosov Moscow State University.

Serbia

- Slavko Alčaković, Associate Professor of Digital Marketing, Sports Marketing, and Gaming at Singidunum University.

Singapore

- Shefaly Shorey, Associate Professor, Alice Lee Centre for Nursing Studies, Yong Loo Lin School of Medicine, National University of Singapore.

Spain

- Marta Hernández-Arriaza, Research Assistant, Faculty of Humanities and Social Sciences, Pontifical Comillas University.

- Gonzalo Aza Blanc, Associate Professor of Psychology, Faculty of Humanities and Social Sciences, Pontifical Comillas University.
- Isabel Muñoz San Roque, Professor of Education, Faculty of Humanities and Social Sciences, Pontifical Comillas University.

Turkey

- İsmail Hakkı Tekiner, Department of Food and Nutrition, Istanbul Sabahattin Zaim University, Türkiye; Ansbach University of Applied Sciences, Germany.

United Arab Emirates

- Nisreen Ameen, Lecturer in Marketing at Royal Holloway, University of London.

United Kingdom

- Jayne Aldridge, Director for the Student Experience at the University of Sussex.

We would also like to thank the hundreds of institutional and organizational liaisons worldwide who distributed the survey. Mostly, though, we want to extend our gratitude to the Gen Zers who took the time to share their thoughts, opinions, and voices with us.

Chapter 1

Introduction

Corey Seemiller[a] *and Meghan Grace*[b]

[a]Wright State University, USA
[b]Plaid, LLC, USA

Abstract

This chapter offers information about the formation of the peer personality
of generations, with a specific focus on the global peer personality of Generation Z as found in the Global Gen Z Study. An explanation of the study's
data collection procedures, including existing validated scales used within the
survey, and data analysis methods, including the use of regionally disaggregated groups from the World Values Survey (World Values Survey
Association, 2022), is discussed.

Keywords: Peer personality; generations; global; world values; cultural
influences; generational cohort

Loyal, Compassionate, and Open-minded. These are just some of the self-described
characteristics of Generation Z, those born from 1995 to 2010. Members of Generation Z have a unique set of attributes, experiences, preferences, and expectations
that impact how they navigate the world. This book showcases the context within
which Gen Zers from around the world have come of age and what we need to know
to best engage, mentor, support, and supervise them to leverage their potential for
success.

The Concept of Generational Research

The study of generations offers a unique look at trends in attitudes and behaviors
of individuals based on age and stage in life. Liken to studies that disaggregate by
gender, religion, or race that aim to understand values, behaviors, and perspectives of social identity groups, generational research provides insight in helping

Gen Z Around the World, 1–9
Copyright © 2024 Corey Seemiller and Meghan Grace
Published under exclusive licence by Emerald Publishing Limited
doi:10.1108/978-1-83797-092-620241001

uncover a peer personality of a group of individuals who share a demographic commonality based on the timeframe in which they are born. In this case, generational cohorts progress through childhood, adolescence, and adulthood at the same time, experiencing current events and societal influences during the same stage of life. These experiences contribute to the creation of a peer personality, which can result in members having similar attitudes, preferences, styles, and behaviors (Seemiller & Grace, 2019).

Identifying why differences emerge between generations is the first step in being able to understand the peer personality of a group. For example, what factors, societal events, or influences during one's adolescence and young adulthood may have impacted how different generations approach civic engagement, develop views on diversity, retain in the workplace, or engage in particular spending behaviors? By understanding what has shaped one's experience during a formative time of human development, it may be easier to appreciate and embrace generational differences and provide a context that can help in making larger scale decisions regarding policy, practices, curriculum development, programs, and initiatives that target an entire demographic of individuals.

Global Peer Personality

In looking at peer personality at the global level, themes can develop that help describe the global cohort culture of Generation Z. This is significant in that there is a lack of large-scale, coordinated global research, nation-specific studies using various methodologies, which create difficulties in comparing data, and there is a growing sense of global interdependence which makes the events and influences impacting Generation Z more homogenous.

Lack of Global Research

While Generation Z has received a great deal of attention in both scholarly publications and mainstream media, there is still limited research in understanding this demographic, particularly on a global level. Most research on Generation Z has come from the United States. For example, Twenge (2017) wrote her book, iGen, using a large-scale dataset from the United States. In addition, much research about Generation Z comes from the Pew Research Center, specifically focused on the United States (Parker & Igielnik, 2020), and even a cursory online search shows that many of the more widely known books on Generation Z are written by American authors.

While research on this generation has become more widespread in the United States, scholars in other countries have recently been conducting their own research (e.g., McCrindle, n.d., in Australia; Redmond, n.d., in the United Kingdom; Sakdiyakorn et al., 2021, in Thailand; Global News, 2018, in Canada; and Ordun et al., 2021, in Turkey). However, research is scant among a variety of other countries, leaving scholars and practitioners the need to reference data from other countries.

Different Methods Across Studies

Further, when studies are undertaken in various nations, they are often conducted independently by researchers studying young people in their respective countries using methodologies and survey questions vastly different from those used in other studies. While the findings from a country's independent study can be useful from a national perspective, comparing populations across studies can be more challenging. In addition, various studies with nuanced methodologies might be helpful for triangulating data and deriving thematic findings, but the differences in approaches do not allow for true comparison.

Greater Global Interdependence

The world is also becoming increasingly interdependent, resulting in the development of a much stronger global peer personality of Generation Z. Perhaps the similarities are due to the ever-expanding "era of technology and communication," which is resulting in greater worldwide accessibility to the internet (Wargadinata et al., 2020, p. 142) or globalization in which multinational companies, nearly geographically limitless tech platforms, and constant travel and contact make it easier than ever to share some element of modern culture that cuts across a multitude of nations.

Further, the COVID-19 pandemic accelerated globalization as health, trade, economies, and the labor force were all interconnected and necessitated a coordinated response (Sforza & Steininger, 2020). And, the general response to communication and learning globally has included more online synchronous and asynchronous learning with an increased reliance on digital resources in place of face-to-face interaction (Ferri et al., 2020). Thus, learning about Generation Z from a global perspective can expand our understanding to better work with, engage, supervise, and educate young people across our interconnected world.

Global Gen Z Study

In February 2021, Seemiller and Grace compiled survey questions for a study on Generation Z. The original intent was to deploy this study as a follow-on to their 2014 study published in Generation Z Goes to College (Seemiller & Grace, 2016) using many of the same measurements and methods but expanding the instrument to include more contemporary topics not included in 2014.

Instrument

The survey included 35 quantitative questions and six qualitative questions. Aside from demographics, survey measurements reflected characteristics, learning preferences, pandemic behaviors, social issues of concern, relationships, civic engagement activities, social media and communication preferences, and political actions.

Similar to the 2014 study, five measurements from the Life Orientation Test (Scheier et al., 1994) were included to measure optimism, although two measurements were slightly adapted. However, in 2021, a newly added aggregate composite score was used to better understand Generation Z's overall level of optimism.

In addition, measurements from the Motivation Indicator (Seemiller, 2009) were incorporated to assess the extent to which participants find various motivators useful, as was used in 2014. The 22 motivators fall into three categories: Eight extrinsic, seven relational, and seven intrinsic.

Collaborators

After finalizing the survey instrument, Seemiller and Grace started reaching out to potential research collaborators from around the world based on a search on Google Scholar and Research Gate in regard to who was publishing about Generation Z. Many had published books and articles on the topic, specific to their disciplines, and were the foremost experts on Generation Z research in their respective countries.

After inviting more than 50 scholars from around the world, 30 confirmed their participation as research partners and assembled their own research teams in their respective countries, resulting in a larger global team of 91 researchers. Their disciplines included marketing, nutrition, psychology, higher education, leadership, engineering, food enginomics/sustainability, youth culture, design, world languages, literature, public health, tourism, transculturality/gender studies, rehabilitation, childhood education, sports/culture/events, pedagogy, management, foreign trade/commerce, theology, human resource management, family studies, political science, management information systems, economics/international cooperation, physical education, journalism, entrepreneurship, digital marketing, and humanities. The expansive list of fields of study these researchers represent is critical for understanding a cohort from a multifaceted perspective. These disciplines in their own ways draw on a knowledge base that connects to understanding, from various lenses, the societal events that have shaped Generation Z.

Cultural Adaptation

Each research partner was provided with the survey questions and asked to adapt them to culturally align with the values and norms of their geographic region. For example, the choices offered for the political ideologies measurement were changed to represent political parties and affiliations relevant to each country. In addition to cultural adaptations, some countries opted to deploy the survey in English while others translated the survey into their native language(s). The survey was ultimately offered in 19 different languages. From a research design perspective, offering the survey in a prominent language used in each country demonstrates a level of cultural responsiveness that encourages participation.

Each research partner sent the survey link to their networks in their countries to solicit participation. Most outreach took place through higher education institutions with the target audience being undergraduate college students. The link was shared on social media, through listservs, in newsletters, and through direct outreach.

Participants

Between the end of September 2021 and the beginning of January 2022, 21,377 Gen Z participants completed the survey from the 32 participating countries. Participants from an additional 49 write-in countries also completed the survey, yielding representation from 81 countries in total. The demographics of the study are included in Table 1.1.

While the main focus of this book is to describe the global aggregate peer personality of Generation Z, it can still be informative to disaggregate the data into regional groupings. For one, understanding if and to what extent cultural nuances shape survey responses can help shed light on where any differences might exist, both geographically and with specific topics. Second, disaggregating the data can provide the opportunity for a comparative analysis, which could in turn showcase the strength of the aggregate global findings. For example, if, when disaggregated, most or even all regional groupings have the same finding on a measurement, there may be more assurance of the universality of the aggregate global finding.

World Values Regions

Although geographic groupings were considered for disaggregation, the cultural, social, economic, and religious nuances can differ drastically from countries that share a border. Thus, division by geography was not viewed by the researchers as the most compelling way to analyze disaggregated groupings. Instead, the World Values Regions were used as an analytical framework as this model using a distinct clustering of countries based on beliefs that impact socioeconomic development, with the rationale that some countries, even geographically distant from one another, have more in common from a values perspective than perhaps nearby countries in the region (World Values Survey Association, 2022).

Ronald Inglehart and Christian Weizel developed a cultural map that plots a variety of countries into separate regions based on the extent of each country's traditional versus secular values as well as survival versus self-expression values. Traditional values are tied to high levels of religious identification and nationalism. Secular values are less grounded in religion and more in traditional social institutions. Survival values are those related to having security and are connected to ethnocentrism and lower trust, whereas self-expression values are reflective of inclusion and the democratic process (World Values Survey Association, 2022).

Table 1.2 includes the participating countries in the Global Generation Z Study and their placement in the Inglehart–Weizel World Cultural Map 2022.

Table 1.1. Demographics of the Global Gen Z Study.

	Percent
Gender	
Woman	65%
Man	31%
Nonbinary	2%
Other	2%
Race	
White	70%
Asian/Asian-American	8%
Hispanic/Latino	7%
Black/African-American	5%
Native/Indigenous	2%
Middle Eastern	2%
Other	6%
Religion	
Participate in organized religion	39%
Spiritual, but not religious	30%
Not spiritual or religious	30%
College student	94%
Business major	24%
Social science major	13%
Health and medicine major	11%
Education/family and human development major	10%
Engineering, technology, and computer science major	10%
Other major	32%

It's important to note that while all regions are included in this book for comparative analysis, some regions had low numbers of participants. These include Africa with 30 participants and West and South Asia with 51. Further, not all countries in the World Values Regions (World Values Survey Association, 2022) were included in this study, making some regions like Confucian, Latin America, Protestant Europe, and West and South Asia perhaps not generalizable to other nonrepresented countries in those regions. While these limitations may influence some of the more nuanced findings, it is clear that the similarities across many regions around a variety of topics discussed in this book provide strong validity for a global peer personality of Generation Z.

Table 1.2. World Values Regions and Participating Countries.

World Values Region	N	Traditional Versus Secular	Survival Versus Self-Expression
*Africa	30	Unknown	Unknown
+Botswana	30		
African-Islamic	3,358	Lean traditional	Lean survival
Turkey	808		
India	285		
Indonesia	628		
Jordan	271		
+United Arab Emirates	309		
+Israel	625		
+Lebanon	432		
Catholic Europe	3,658	Lean secular	Lean self-expression
Italy	269		
Portugal	540		
Spain	1,455		
Austria	1,241		
Belgium	153		
Confucian	482	Secular	In-between
Hong Kong	4		
China	478		
English-Speaking	6,589	Lean secular	Self-expression
The United States	5,170		
Australia	272		
The United Kingdom	1,050		
+Canada	97		
Latin America	1,494	Lean traditional	In-between
Brazil	909		
Ecuador	53		
Philippines	532		
Orthodox Europe	3,668	Lean secular	Lean survival
Bulgaria	861		
Russia	268		

(Continued)

Table 1.2. *(Continued)*

World Values Region	*N*	Traditional Versus Secular	Survival Versus Self-Expression
Serbia	200		
Romania	1,654		
Cyprus	130		
Montenegro	555		
Protestant Europe	1868	Secular	Self-expression
Germany	1,630		
The Netherlands	238		
West and South Asia	51	In-between	In-between
Singapore	51		

Note: Participating countries from the Global Gen Z Study (Seemiller & Grace, 2019) marked with an + were not included in the World Values Survey but were listed in this table based on the authors' determination of their best placement, given their espoused societal values. The region entitled Africa, which is marked with a *, is a category constructed by the authors for Botswana and is not a World Values Survey region, because presumed placement of Botswana into the existing regions was more difficult.

Data Analysis

In January 2022, after the completion of data collection, research partners were sent the data from their respective countries. Further, collaboration groups were formed to analyze the entire global dataset, ultimately resulting in the development of this book. Simple frequency counts and percentages were used to look at larger scale trends of the quantitative data, and thematic coding was used to analyze the open-ended questions.

Conclusion

Members of Generation Z are our children, students, coworkers, neighbors, congregants, patients, constituents, clients, customers, supervisees, team members, advisees, and loved ones. And, only when we can better understand how to connect and engage with this global cohort can we tap into the potential they have to make the world a better place for all of us.

References

Ferri, F., Grifoni, P., & Guzzo, T. (2020). Online learning and emergency remote teaching: Opportunities and challenges in emergency situations. *Societies, 10*(86). https://doi.org/10.3390/soc10040086

Global News. (2018). *Generation Z: Canada's untapped generation*. https://globalnews.ca/tag/generation-z/

Inglehart, R., & Welzel, C. (2022). *The Inglehart-Welzel World Cultural Map – World Values Survey 7*. http://www.worldvaluessurvey.org/

McCrindle. (n.d). *Everything you ever wanted to know about Gen Z*. https://generationz.com.au/

Ordun, G., Özveren, C. G., & Mercimek, K. (2021). Social, cultural, emotional intelligence and entrepreneurial intention: A research on Generation Z. *Journal of Organizational Behavior Review*, *3*(2), 222–240.

Parker, K., & Igielnik, R. (2020). *On the cusp of adulthood and facing an uncertain future: What we know about Gen Z so far*. https://www.pewresearch.org/social-trends/2020/05/14/on-the-cusp-of-adulthood-and-facing-an-uncertain-future-what-we-know-about-gen-z-so-far-2/

Redmond, P. (n.d.). *Mind the generation gap*. https://www.paul-redmond.co.uk/

Sakdiyakorn, M., Golubovskaya, M., & Solnet, D. (2021). Understanding Generation Z through collective consciousness: Impacts for hospitality work and employment. *International Journal of Hospitality Management*, *94*, 102822. https://doi.org/10.1016/j.ijhm.2020.102822

Scheier, M. F., Carver, C. S., & Bridges, M. W. (1994). Distinguishing optimism from neuroticism (and trait anxiety, self-mastery, and self-esteem): A re-evaluation of the Life Orientation Test. *Journal of Personality and School Psychology*, *67*(7), 1063–1078.

Seemiller, C. (2009). *Motivation indicator*. The University of Arizona. Unpublished manuscript.

Seemiller, C., & Grace, M. (2016). *Generation Z goes to college*. Jossey-Bass.

Seemiller, C., & Grace, M. (2019). *Generation Z: A century in the making*. Routledge.

Sforza, A., & Steininger, M. (2020). *Globalization in the time of COVID-19*. Munich Society for the Promotion of Economic Research – CESifo GmbH. ISSN 2364-1428.

Twenge, J. M. (2017). *iGen: Why today's super-connected kids are growing up less rebellious, more tolerant, less happy—and completely unprepared for adulthood—and what that means for the rest of us*. Atria Books.

Wargadinata, I., Maimunah, I., Dewi, E., & Rofiq, Z. (2020). Student's responses on learning in the early COVID-19 pandemic. *Tadris: Journal of Education and Teacher Training*, *5*(1), 141–153. https://doi.org/10.24042/tadris.v5i1.6153

World Values Survey Association. (2022). *World values survey*. https://www.worldvaluessurvey.org/WVSContents.jsp

Chapter 2

Characteristics and Motivations

Meghan Grace[a] *and Corey Seemiller*[b]

[a]Plaid, LLC, USA
[b]Wright State University, USA

Abstract

Like every generation before them, Gen Zers possess a specific set of attributes. For example, they identify as loyal, thoughtful, compassionate, and responsible. They share their sense of ingenuity and resourcefulness with their Gen X parental generation and embrace diversity and inclusion like their older millennial counterparts. And, they connect with their baby boomer grandparents with their shared sense of responsibility. Generation Z is motivated by achievement and making a difference. Although some believe others will let them down, the majority are optimistic about their futures and believe good things will happen for them.

Keywords: Characteristics; motivations; optimism; diversity; attributes; generations

Because each generational cohort can have different characteristics and be motivated in unique ways, knowing these can be foundational for understanding and effectively working together. This is particularly poignant in that characteristics and motivations can impact the way individuals communicate, learn, engage, and navigate the world as they can underpin how and why people behave. In looking at Generation Z, it becomes apparent that uncovering how they describe themselves and what drives them is paramount for understanding how this cohort behaves in other areas of their lives.

Characteristics

Characteristics are studied to better define generational cohorts and their distinct peer personalities beyond social identity demographics, such as race, gender,

Gen Z Around the World, 11–20
Copyright © 2024 Meghan Grace and Corey Seemiller
Published under exclusive licence by Emerald Publishing Limited
doi:10.1108/978-1-83797-092-620241002

religion, or place of residence. Generation Z has been described as loyal, compassionate, thoughtful, open-minded, responsible, and determined (Seemiller & Grace, 2016) and collaborative, flexible, authentic, social, and pragmatic (De Witte, 2022).

To gain clarity on the global peer personality of the Generation Z cohort, participants in the Global Gen Z Study were asked to select, "Does not describe me," "Somewhat describes me," or "Greatly describes me" for 35 different descriptors. In looking at the percentages of participants who selected "Greatly describes me" for each characteristic, a ranking of all 35 occurred. Table 2.1 includes the five highest percentages and the five lowest.

The top characteristics of the Global Gen Z population align with the findings from a past study on Generation Z (Seemiller & Grace, 2016) in which US Gen Zers selected loyal, responsible, thoughtful, compassionate, and open-minded as the top characteristics to describe themselves. While the past study only engaged participants in the US (Seemiller & Grace, 2016), the global study presents a much larger and more diverse representation of Generation Z. The similar findings between the two studies provide greater confirmation of the self-identified characteristics that can be used to describe Generation Z as a cohort, especially as the global population engaged a cohort of participants beyond those predominantly based in the US.

In addition, it is clear how Gen Zers do not describe themselves – forward-thinking characteristics like visionary and inspiring, competition-based characteristics like opportunistic and competitive, as well as the more traditional characteristic of conservative, which stands in stark opposition to the more progressive-minded characteristic of open-minded that ranks in the top five.

When examining Generation Z by World Values Regions (World Values Survey Association, 2022), some differences emerge in how Gen Zers around the world view and describe themselves. These are showcased in Table 2.2.

Gen Zers overwhelmingly view themselves as loyal, with this characteristic being the top cited one in seven of the eight regions, although it was still high-ranking as the second highest in the Confucian region. Loyalty was the only characteristic present in the top five in each world region.

Of the global top five characteristics (loyal, responsible, thoughtful, compassionate, and open-minded), responsible and thoughtful were included in seven of the nine regions as top characteristics, and compassionate and open-minded were found in five of the nine regions as top characteristics.

Table 2.1. Characteristics.

Greatly Describes Me		Does Not Describe Me	
Loyal	77%	Conservative	42%
Responsible	64%	Opportunistic	24%
Thoughtful	63%	Competitive	23%
Compassionate	62%	Visionary	20%
Open-minded	61%	Inspiring	19%

Table 2.2. Top 5 Characteristics by Region.

Region	#1	#2	#3	#4	#5
Africa[a]	Loyal (83%)	Realistic (81%)	Open-minded (71%)	Compassionate (71%)	Thoughtful (70%)
African-Islamic	Loyal (76%)	Compassionate (65%)	Responsible (64%)	Open-minded (63%)	Thoughtful (61%)
Catholic Europe	Loyal (82%)	Responsible (65%)	Curious (65%)	Open-minded (64%)	Authentic (62%)
Confucian	Responsible (51%)	Loyal (46%)	Authentic (44%)	Optimistic (42%)	Unique (40%)
English-Speaking	Loyal (76%)	Thoughtful (71%)	Compassionate (66%)	Open-minded (63%)	Responsible (61%)
Latin America	Loyal (77%)	Open-minded (74%)	Thoughtful (67%)	Cooperative (62%)	Curious (61%)
Orthodox Europe	Loyal (77%)	Responsible (67%)	Realistic (62%)	Sensible (61%)	Thoughtful (60%)
Protestant Europe	Loyal (78%)	Responsible (73%)	Thoughtful (70%)	Compassionate (70%)	Curious (64%)
West and South Asia	Loyal (81%)	Compassionate (77%)	Thoughtful (74%)	Responsible (72%)	Open-minded (70%)

[a]Not included in the World Values Survey.

The presence of these characteristics in some regions and not in other regions accentuates the notion that Generation Z as a global cohort possesses a lot of similarity in identity while recognizing that geographic region can play a role in how Gen Zers see and describe themselves. For one, the Confucian region garnered the most unique characteristics list compared to other regions as it was only one of two regions in which authentic was among the top five and the only region to include optimistic and unique. Additionally, the Latin America region was the only one to have cooperative in the top five and was only one of three regions to have curious included in its list. As a region, Latin America leans toward traditional values, which focus on religious faith and respect for authority (World Values Survey Association, 2022), which likely aligns with Gen Zers seeing themselves as cooperative. However, Latin America also falls in between survival and self-expressive values, which may be driving why Gen Zers in this region identify as curious, both out of a need for finding solutions to maintain their security and because of their value of cultural acceptance (World Values Survey Association, 2022). Orthodox Europe is the only region to include realistic and sensible in its list of top characteristics, which may be linked to the region's lean toward survival values, which focus on aspiring toward economic and physical security (World Values Association, 2022).

Motivations

While understanding characteristics of a generation helps to illuminate how a cohort views and describes themselves, understanding their motivations can help explain why they may engage in various actions or behaviors.

Motivation is the energy or drive an individual possesses in order to take a specific action or engage in a behavior or set of behaviors (Earl & Hall, 2018; Pinder, 2014). The concept of motivation can be conceptualized as one of three types: intrinsic, extrinsic, and relational. Intrinsic motivation encourages behavior that leads to inherent enjoyment or a sense of accomplishment, whereas extrinsic motivation draws from sources that lead to an external outcome or benefit (Pinder, 2014). Sources of relational motivation are those in which motivation is linked to positively impacting other people (Seemiller, 2009).

To measure motivation, the Global Gen Z Study prompted participants to rate various forms of motivation by selecting from the options, "Does not motivate me," "Somewhat motivates me," and "Greatly motivates me." The framework utilized to measure motivation is drawn from the motivation indicator (Seemiller, 2009), which measures 22 sources of motivation that can be categorized into eight extrinsic, seven relational, and seven intrinsic motivators. The sources of motivation are outlined in Table 2.3.

Table 2.4 includes the five motivation sources with the highest percentages and five with the lowest percentages of "Greatly motivates me" as reported by Gen Zers in the Global Gen Z Study.

Three of the top five sources of motivation are intrinsic sources of motivation; one is extrinsic and the other is relational. This lean toward intrinsic motivation

Table 2.3. Sources of Motivation.

Intrinsic	Extrinsic	Relational
Learning something or being better at something	Receiving tangible rewards *(scholarships, awards, prizes, gifts, money)*	Not wanting to let others down
Seeing the fruits of your labor/ accomplishment	Earning credit toward something *(academic credit or completing requirements toward something larger)*	Being accepted by others
Wanting to do well because you committed	Gaining experience to build your resume	Feeling the need to be loyal to the values of your community
Competing with yourself	Avoiding penalties *(fines, loss of privileges)*	Making a difference for someone else
Caring about the project or task	Receiving public recognition	Pleasing others *(impress or appease family or friends)*
Advocating for something you believe in	Competing with others to win	Receiving individual recognition
Wanting to leave a legacy	Knowing that someone may return the favor	Achieving or maintaining status or credibility
	Having an opportunity for advancement *(promotion, new opportunities)*	

indicates that Generation Z as a global cohort is driven by forms of motivation that are focused on activities that bring them fulfillment, accomplishment, enjoyment, or align with their passions. This is exhibited by their strong gravitation toward being motivated by seeing the fruits of your labor or accomplishments, advocating for something you believe in, and learning something or being better at something. These results align with those from Kirchmayer and Fratričová (2018) who found that accomplishment is one of the most prevalent factors in motivating Generation Z. In addition, a previous study by Seemiller and Grace (2016) found US Gen Zers being motivated by passion and achievement.

Given the preponderance of intrinsic motivators, Gen Zers appear to be more driven by achievement of personal, professional, and societal goals as opposed to extrinsically driven by competing with others, knowing that others may return the

Table 2.4. Motivation Sources.

Greatly Motivated By		Does Not Motivate	
Seeing the fruits of your labor or accomplishments (Intrinsic)	70%	Competing with others to win (Extrinsic)	33%
Having an opportunity for advancement (Extrinsic)	66%	Knowing that others may return the favor (Extrinsic)	28%
Advocating for something you believe in (Intrinsic)	65%	Wanting to leave a legacy (Intrinsic)	25%
Learning something or being better at something (Intrinsic)	65%	Receiving public recognition (Extrinsic)	25%
Not wanting to let others down (Relational)	63%	Being accepted by others (Relational)	22%

favor, and public recognition, which garnered some of the lowest percentages of "Greatly motivates me."

It should be noted that what appears to motivate Gen Zers may be due to their current life stage. Many are students or new employees early in their careers where it would make sense that they would be focused on self-improvement, growth, and personal contributions rather than drawing attention to themselves through competition, leaving a legacy, trading favors, seeking acceptance, or recognition.

A more nuanced analysis of motivations, on the other hand, indicates variations among regions with Gen Zers around the world. Table 2.5 highlights each region's highest percentages for "Greatly motivates me."

Like the similarities across the globe with Generation Z's characteristics, there too is little variation by region with sources of motivation. For example, seeing the fruits of your labor or accomplishments, which is listed in the global top five, is also present in every region's top five sources of motivation. This motivation source may have a tie to Gen Zers' views of themselves as loyal and responsible as both of those characteristics reflect consistency, a sense of obligation, and remaining committed to something or someone.

In addition, having an opportunity for advancement is listed as a top five motivation source in seven of the nine regions. The prominence of this motivation is not surprising considering other research has found that advancement opportunities are critical for Generation Z employees, in particular (Perna, 2021).

Further, Perna (2021) points out that Gen Zers crave learning and development opportunities, which aligns with five of the nine regions that included learning something or being better at something as a top five motivator. A common thread in four of the five regions that include learning something or being better at something as a top five source of motivation is having secular values or leaning toward secular values. According to the World Values Survey

Table 2.5. Top Five Sources of Motivation by Region.

Region	Sources of Motivation
Africa[a]	Seeing the fruits of your labor or accomplishments (83%) Wanting to leave a legacy (77%) Making a difference for someone else (75%) Caring about the project or task (74%) Having an opportunity for advancement (74%) Wanting to do well because you committed (74%)
African-Islamic	Having an opportunity for advancement (77%) Seeing the fruits of your labor or accomplishments (77%) Learning something or being better at something (73%) Wanting to do well because you committed (69%) Gaining experience to build your resume (68%)
Catholic Europe	Seeing the fruits of your labor or accomplishments (77%) Advocating for something you believe in (71%) Learning something or being better at something (67%) Having an opportunity for advancement (66%) Wanting to do well because you committed (64%)
Confucian	Having an opportunity for advancement (57%) Seeing the fruits of your labor or accomplishments (52%) Receiving public recognition (47%) Receiving individual recognition (46%) Gaining experience to build your resume (45%)
English-Speaking	Not wanting to let others down (72%) Making a difference for someone else (64%) Advocating for something you believe in (62%) Seeing the fruits of your labor or accomplishments (61%) Having an opportunity for advancement (60%)
Latin America	Seeing the fruits of your labor or accomplishments (82%) Having an opportunity for advancement (81%) Learning something or being better at something (74%) Receiving tangible rewards (68%) Wanting to do well because you committed (68%)

(Continued)

Table 2.5. *(Continued)*

Region	Sources of Motivation
Orthodox Europe	Seeing the fruits of your labor or accomplishments (78%) Having an opportunity for advancement (76%) Learning something or being better at something (67%) Advocating for something you believe in (66%) Wanting to do well because you committed (63%)
Protestant Europe	Making a difference for someone else (71%) Pleasing others (71%) Not wanting to let others down (71%) Seeing the fruits of your labor or accomplishments (66%) Learning something or being better at something (66%)
West and South Asia	Seeing the fruits of your labor or accomplishments (79%) Not wanting to let others down (74%) Wanting to do well because you committed (72%) Making a difference for someone else (72%) Having an opportunity for advancement (72%)

[a]Not included in the World Values Survey.

Association (2022), regions with secular values prioritize children learning independence and determination. The African-Islamic region also included learning something or being better at something as a source of motivation, but this may be more driven by the survival-leaning values that prioritize aspiring toward economic security which may be enhanced by learning and personal growth.

Additionally, advocating for something you believe in is present in the Orthodox Europe, Catholic Europe, and English-Speaking regions, all of which are labeled as lean secular in their values sets (World Values Survey Association, 2022). These three regions place less emphasis on traditional social institutions, so the drive to engage in advocacy is likely linked to a commitment to improving societal markers of community such as family systems, education and schools, government, religion, and the economy (Nickerson & Mcleod, 2023).

Only five unique top five motivators emerged. These included caring about the project or task (Africa), public recognition (Confucian), individual recognition (Confucian), tangible rewards (Latin America), and pleasing others (Protestant Europe). However, the majority of the motivation sources listed were present across multiple regions.

Conclusion

Understanding the characteristics and motivations of the Generation Z cohort can have multiple benefits. First, knowing how Gen Zers see themselves and what drives them can help others gain a greater appreciation for their perspectives and behaviors, which may foster better interpersonal dynamics. Second, being able to be intentional about connection points with Gen Zers can build and strengthen relationships. For instance, most Gen Zers describe themselves as loyal. Finding ways to interact and connect with them through their sense of loyalty, such as following through, showing up when you say you will, and sticking by them through tough times, will likely go a long way.

From the workplace and education spaces to community organizations and societal movements, understanding what motivates a generation can help others create pathways that can move them to action. Insight into their motivations can help educators, leaders, and employers better engage this global cohort to reach their goals and the goals of organizations. For example, knowing that most Gen Zers are motivated by intrinsic sources, those supervising, advising, or leading them may need to accept that many are best motivated internally and may not resonate generally with many of the extrinsic or relational motivation strategies they might offer, like recognition or competition. However, with one extrinsic and one relational motivator in their top five, specific strategies may work well. For example, incorporating opportunities for advancement as well as clearly explaining why a task is important and who it benefits could go be incredibly motivating for them.

Coupling Generation Z's characteristics with motivations allows for a deeper understanding of this cohort's core values and perspectives. Given both, it appears Generation Z is a cohort that stands by the people and causes they care about and is motivated to achieve great things to make a positive impact.

References

De Witte, M. (2022). *Gen Z are not 'coddled.' They are highly collaborative, self-reliant and pragmatic, according to new Stanford-affiliated research.* https://news.stanford. edu/2022/01/03/know-gen-z/

Earl, A., & Hall, M. P. (2018). Motivational influences on attitudes. In D. Albarracin & B. Johnson (Eds.), *The handbook of attitudes, volume 1: Basic principles* (2nd ed., pp. 377–403). Taylor & Francis.

Kirchmayer, Z., & Fratričová, J. (2018). What motivates Generation Z at work? Insights into motivation drivers of business students in Slovakia. In *31st IBIMA conference, Italy, Vol. Innovation management and education excellence through vision 2020* (pp. 6019–6030). https://www.researchgate.net/publication/335569679_ Innovation_Management_and_Education_Excellence_through_Vision_2020

Nickerson, C., & Mcleod, S. (2023). *Social institutions in sociology: Definition and examples.* https://simplysociology.com/social-institution.html

Perna, M. C. (2021). *Why skill and career advancement are the way to Gen-Z's heart.* https://www.forbes.com/sites/markcperna/2021/03/02/why-skill-and-career-advancement-are-the-way-to-gen-zs-heart/?sh=1828b17722b5

Pinder, C. (2014). *Work motivation in organizational behavior* (2nd ed.). Taylor & Francis.

Seemiller, C. (2009). *Motivation indicator.* The University of Arizona. Unpublished manuscript.

Seemiller, C., & Grace, M. (2016). *Generation Z goes to college.* Jossey-Bass.

World Values Survey Association. (2022). *World values survey.* https://www.worldvaluessurvey.org/WVSContents.jsp

Chapter 3

Happiness and Outlook

Niva Dolev[a], Eman Tarabia[a] and Keba T. Modisane[b]

[a]Kinneret College on the Sea of Galilee, Israel
[b]Basikwa Holdings-Women & Youth Entrepreneurship & Empowerment
(PTY) Ltd, Botswana

Abstract

The pursuit of happiness as a fundamental human goal is an ancient and widely discussed concept. Recent studies have noted that Gen Zers experience higher levels of stress than previous generations. At the same time, findings of the global study show that while Gen Zers are not overly optimistic, they are realistic, somewhat flexible and adaptable to situations, socially connected, and engaged and committed to making a difference in the world. While these qualities may at least partly mitigate stress levels and contribute to Gen Z's happiness, resilience should be cultivated in Gen Z.

Keywords: Happiness; optimism; adaptability; meaning; resilience; interpersonal relationships

The pursuit of happiness as a fundamental human goal has been widely discussed by philosophers, even in early times (Judge & Kammeyer-Mueller, 2011). Its scientific study, however, has emerged only more recently, often interwoven with the study of subjective well-being (Oishi et al., 2013). According to Diener (2000), happiness, positive affect, and life satisfaction all contribute to one's well-being. While there is currently a growing understanding of its importance (Seligman, 2011) as demonstrated by the yearly Happy Planet Index (HPI) first introduced in 2006, the concept of happiness has remained relatively elusive (Oishi et al., 2013).

Happiness is a universal virtue. It is defined as an emotional state that fluctuates with life events and experiences (Modisane, 2023). According to the Authentic Happiness theory (Seligman, 2004), positive emotions, engagement, and meaning contribute to happiness levels (Scorsolini-Comin et al., 2013). Hedonists describe happiness as having more positive experiences, pleasant feelings, and favorable choices

Gen Z Around the World, 21–29
Copyright © 2024 Niva Dolev, Eman Tarabia and Keba T. Modisane
Published under exclusive licence by Emerald Publishing Limited
doi:10.1108/978-1-83797-092-620241003

than negative ones, and draw on sense of life satisfaction (Lower, 2014; Ryan & Deci, 2001). From a Eudaimonic viewpoint, happiness is exacted from actualizing one's potential, finding meaning in life, and utilizing one's virtues (Scorsolini-Comin et al., 2013).

Happiness, in turn, increases the perception of social connectedness and the adoption of a positive lifestyle, and contributes to positive functioning (Kok & Fredrickson, 2010), including at work (Argyle, 2013). It also contributes to the tendency to help others, to engage in flexible thinking and to produce solutions for problems (Isen & Geva, 1987). Having a meaningful life, a Eudaimonic aspect of being happy, is related to self-acceptance, positive relations, autonomy, environmental mastery, and purpose in life (Ryff, 2008). In her broaden-and-build theory, Fredrickson (2013) further suggested that happiness broadens possibilities and widens thought.

History and culture were found to influence happiness levels (Joshanloo, 2014; Oishi et al., 2013), suggesting that generational differences are likely to have a role in happiness levels (Smaliukiene & Bekesiene, 2020). As the ability to be happy is critical for well-being, understanding influences and perceptions of Gen Zers' happiness is of great importance.

Stress Tolerance

Stress is known to endanger one's happiness levels and combat the ability to experience happiness and other positive feelings (Selye, 1976). Levels of stress and anxiety are on the rise (Goleman, 2020), with Gen Zers experiencing higher levels than previous generations (Jacobs, 2022). This increased stress contributes to depression, addiction, loneliness, suicidal thoughts, and self-harm (Jacobs, 2022). Furthermore, the ability to manage stress is the lowest among Generation Z compared to previous generations (American Psychological Association, 2020). And while this may seem like a concerning trend, it should also be noted that the awareness, recognition, treatment, and documentation of mental health concerns is greater today than it was for previous generations at similar life stages.

During their teen and young adult years, Gen Zers witnessed global and local adversities, such as the 2008/2009 economic recession and its aftermath, ongoing international conflicts, vast immigration waves, public shootings and terror attacks, and natural disasters, all of which negatively impacted Generation Z's stress levels (Seemiller & Grace, 2016).

Gen Zers may also be experiencing stress currently stemming from the need to enter the organizational world with less experience than previous generations, due to fewer work opportunities for teens (Cucina et al., 2018). The recent COVID-19 pandemic (Helliwell et al., 2021; Jacobs, 2022), intensified by the high accessibility to information mainly via social media (Seemiller & Grace, 2019), added to their stress levels. Lastly, Generation Z feels stressed about the future and its challenges (APA, 2020) as they face issues such as a growing population density (Sladek & Grabinger, 2014), diseases, and less financial security (Deloitte, 2022b). In particular, Gen Zers are experiencing stress related to environmental issues such as climate change and sustainability, with a growing number of Gen Zers reporting experiencing climate change anxiety (Reyes et al., 2021).

Interestingly, Gen Zers themselves are aware of their generation's stress levels (Veluchamy et al., 2016), and tend to talk of their fears and anxiety rather than hide them (Sladek & Grabinger, 2014), thus engaging in coping mechanisms that help regulate difficult emotions and mitigate stress levels (Stein & Book, 2011).

Adaptability and Resilience

Gen Zers are operating in a world typified by a volatile, uncertain, complex, and ambiguous (VUCA) reality (Johansen & Euchner, 2013). Among the many present challenges are the constant updating of technologies (Reis et al., 2019), unstable work conditions and new modes of employment (Deloitte, 2022a, 2020b), and changes in the nature and requirements of many professions (Dolev & Itzkovich, 2020; McKinsey Global Institute, 2017) as they engage in an increasingly competitive, interconnected, multigenerational, and multicultural reality.

While change may typically be considered a source of stress, adaptability, which is a person's capability and willingness to change, is positively associated with happiness (Öztemel & Yıldız-Akyol, 2021). And, Gen Zers are positioned to adapt to these changes as they are digital natives (Sladek & Grabinger, 2014) who are eager to adopt new technologies (Pew Research Center, 2018); embrace and pursue new modes of employment, such as the gig economy (Deloitte, 2022a); have an economically aware mindset (Sladek & Grabinger, 2014); and prioritize their mental health (Deloitte, 2022b), all of which may have been exacerbated by the global pandemic.

In the Global Gen Z Study, 50% of Gen Zers described themselves as adaptable. Given the timing of this study during the pandemic, it may have been that more young people were compelled to be adaptable to respond to the situation rather than typically identify as adaptable. For example, as a result of the COVID-19 pandemic, 23% looked for a new job, 14% changed career paths, and 52% changed their spending habits.

Resilience, on the other hand, is "the ability to maintain or regain mental health, despite experiencing adversity" (Herrman et al., 2011, p. 259) and may influence Gen Zers' ability to cope with difficulties. Resilience has been found to be a positive correlation of happiness (Lower, 2014). Some researchers have argued that Generation Zers may have low levels of resilience (Harari et al., 2022), which appears to be consistent with findings from the Global Gen Z Study in which only 40% of Gen Zers identify as resilient. However, Ang et al. (2021), in their study, found that Gen Zers may be more resilient than they initially thought or report.

Table 3.1 highlights findings from the Global Gen Z Study for adaptability and resilience, including the regions with the highest and lowest percentages of Gen Zers who indicated that those characteristics greatly described them.

Interestingly, West and South Asia and the English-speaking region have the highest levels of resilience but some of the lowest of adaptability. The Confucian region has the lowest levels of both adaptability and resilience, and other findings were simply scattered. Regardless of regional comparisons, other than perhaps Africa, it is evident that a good number of Gen Zers around the world do not see themselves as either adaptable or resilient, despite having to contend with a constantly changing and challenging reality.

Table 3.1. Adaptability and Resilience.

Characteristic	Global	Percentage that Greatly Describes Them	Percentage that Greatly Describes Them
Adaptable	50%	Africa[a] (64%) African-Islamic (54%) Orthodox Europe (54%)	Confucian (33%) English-Speaking (45%) West and South Asia (45%)
Resilient	40%	West and South Asia (55%) English-Speaking (47%)	Confucian (27%) Protestant Europe (30%)

[a]Not included in the World Values Survey.

Optimism

Optimism is the belief that an individual will experience a greater number of positive rather than negative outcomes and overcome difficulties that emerge. Optimistic people experience happiness and other positive emotions which contribute to their general feeling of happiness. They also tend to act in order to reach their goals (Wani & Dar, 2017) and have better coping mechanisms than unhappy people (Modisane, 2023).

In the Global Gen Z Study, 55% of Gen Zers identified as realistic, which ranked seventh highest out of the 35 choices of characteristics they rated themselves on, whereas only 35% identified as optimistic, which had the 29th highest ranking. Further, optimistic only emerged in the top 10 characteristics for Confucian countries. All other regions listed optimistic lower on the list. Table 3.2 lists the regions with the highest and lowest percentages in both realism and optimism.

What is most striking is that in every region of the world, a far higher percentage of Gen Zers identified as realistic over optimistic.

In looking closer at optimism, though, there are some delineations. For example, the self-reliance aspect of optimism (Seligman, 2004), as expressed in "I am optimistic about my future" (38% agree) and "I believe that good things will happen to me" (37% agree), was greater than their optimism toward others, as expressed in, "I believe people are inherently good (19% agree). Perhaps this stems from what on Gen Zer is calling optimistic pessimism (Given, 2023), in which Gen Zers realize that the world may be falling apart, sometimes at the hands of other generations but that they are hopeful in their part to fix it (Seemiller & Grace, 2019).

Table 3.2. Realism and Optimism.

Characteristic	Global	Percentage That Greatly Describes Them	Percentage That Greatly Describes Them
Realistic	55%	Africa[a] (81%) Orthodox Europe (62%)	Confucian (33%) West and South Asia (43%)
Optimistic	35%	Africa[a] (52%) Latin America (48%)	Protestant Europe (32%) Catholic Europe (33%) Confucian (33%)

[a]Not included in the World Values Survey.

Agency and Pro-Sociality

While some may perceive happiness as being derived as a result of good luck and fortune, that is, emanating from external forces which are not in one's control, viewing happiness as within one's control is actually linked to higher levels of happiness (Oishi et al., 2013). Thus, just the action of chasing happiness may actually lead to happiness.

Gen Zers' concerns about global issues reflect their deep involvement, sense of responsibility, and tenacity to act. In the Global Gen Z Study, 59% indicated that they are greatly motivated, and 34% are somewhat motivated, by knowing that their actions will make a difference for someone else. Engaging in this prosocial behavior, especially when one sees how their help can benefit others, generally promotes happiness (Aknin et al., 2019; Helliwell et al., 2019).

Meaning

Meaning is a critical factor associated with happiness (Seligman, 2011). While meaning can be found in any area of one's life, work offers a space in which some may seek meaning. In their expectations from work, Gen Zers combine two views of happiness, one that is related to the welfare of the collective and one that is related to an individual emotional state (Joshanloo, 2014). In particular, meaning at work and the ability to create change in it are important to Generation Z (SmartCitti, n.d.). In the Global Gen Z Study, Gen Zers shared what they expected of their future jobs describing the importance of interest, meaning, fulfillment and enjoyment, and the ability to influence others and society in general. One Gen Zer said, "What is most important to me in my future career is that I find fulfillment from it. It would be nice if it could provide me with financial stability, but I really hope to enjoy what I do and find meaning in it."

Interpersonal Relationships

Interpersonal relationships and social connections are one of the most important contributors to happiness (Seligman, 2011; Waldinger, 2015). Further, having a sense of belonging and connectedness can help with overcoming difficult times, such as COVID-19 (Dolev et al., 2022).

In particular, the use of social media can be a detractor or contributor to happiness. As a detractor, scholars link technology-based relationships with shallowness, social comparison, and fear of missing out (FOMO), all of which contribute to falling happiness rates (Helliwell et al., 2019). As a contributor, through social media platforms, Gen Zers can join others online anytime and anywhere, thus potentially easing any feelings of loneliness (Helliwell et al., 2021). Gen Zers use platforms like WhatsApp for emotional connection (Katzman et al., 2021).

While social connection can occur using a variety of modalities, spending time in person may be an enhanced form of connection as it provides physical closeness, more nuance through nonverbal communication, opportunities for spontaneous conversations, and effortless communication behaviors (Gruber et al., 2022). These preferences are in line with the results from the Global Gen Z Study in which Gen Zers indicated they most preferred to communicate face-to-face over text, phone calls, and emails. The study also found that Gen Zers engage in a face-to-face communication modality more than any other form of connection.

Even further, Gen Zers perceive well-being at work being linked to social relationships and as a socio-emotional experience (Smaliukiene & Bekesiene, 2020). They value social-emotional intelligence in people over cognitive intelligence (Machová et al., 2020). Similarly, experiencing positive relationships at work emerged as a theme from the Global Gen Z Study qualitative data on what Gen Zers are seeking in their future jobs.

Conclusion

Coupled with literature, the Global Gen Z Survey results have shown that the answer regarding happiness with Gen Z is complex and multifaceted. Gen Zers experience stress and cope with past, present, and future challenges that may negatively impact their happiness levels. They are realistic rather than optimistic about the challenges ahead, and despite how they may view themselves, many had to be adaptable and resilient, dealing with an ever-changing world.

These complex findings call for efforts to promote happiness and positivity in Gen Zers and to modulate negative experiences (Lower, 2014). Parents, educators, and supervisors should take the issue of Generation Z's happiness seriously and help provide opportunities for them to engage in enjoyable, meaningful experiences and interactions as well as cultivate optimism and resilience. This will involve helping them how to identify, use, and share their strengths for their own good and for the benefit of society, and how to bounce back after a challenge. Teaching this generation how to take charge of their own happiness is vital, not just to their happiness but also to their well-being and ability to cope with the present and future challenges of the era.

References

Aknin, L. B., Whillans, A. V., Norton, M. I., & Dunn, E. W. (2019). Happiness and prosocial behavior: An evaluation of the evidence. In J. F. Helliwell, R. Layard, & J. D. Sachs (Eds.), *Happiness global report* (pp. 67–86). Harvard Business School.

American Psychological Association (APA). (2020). *Stress in America 2020*. https://www.apa.org/news/press/releases/stress/2020/report-october

Ang, W. H. D., Shorey, S., Lopez, V., Chew, H. S. J., & Lau, Y. (2021). Generation Z undergraduate students' resilience during the COVID-19 pandemic: A qualitative study. *Current Psychology, 41*, 1–15. https://doi.org/10.1007/s12144-021-01830-4

Argyle, M. (2013). *The psychology of happiness*. Routledge.

Cucina, J. M., Byle, K. A., Martin, N. R., Peyton, S. T., & Gast, I. F. (2018). Generational differences in workplace attitudes and job satisfaction: Lack of sizable differences across cohorts. *Journal of Management Psychology, 33*(3), 246–264. https://doi.org/10.1108/JMP-03-2017-0115

Deloitte. (2022a). Striving for balance, advocating for change. In *The Deloitte global 2022 Gen Z & Millennials survey*. https://www2.deloitte.com/content/dam/Deloitte/global/Documents/deloitte-2022-genz-millennial-survey.pdf

Deloitte. (2022b). *The mental health of Gen Z and Millennials in the new world of work*. https://www2.deloitte.com/content/dam/Deloitte/global/Documents/deloitte-2022-genz-millennial-mh-whitepaper.pdf

Diener, E. (2000). Subjective well-being: The science of happiness and a proposal for a national index. *American Psychologist, 55*(1), 34.

Dolev, N., Amzaleg, M., & Shapira, N. (2022). The hidden part of the iceberg – The impact of social and emotional factors on the links between digital divide and online learning in times of crisis. In B. Katzman, T. Harel, A. Giladi, & M. Koslowsky (Eds.), *Psychological well-being and behavioral interactions during the coronavirus pandemic* (pp. 19–44). Cambridge Scholars Publishing.

Dolev, N., & Itzkovich, Y. (2020). In the AI era, soft skills are the new hard skills. In A. Stachowicz-Stanusch (Ed.), *Management and business education in the time of artificial intelligence* (pp. 55–77). Information Age Publishing.

Fredrickson, B. L. (2013). Positive emotions broaden and build. In P. Devine & A. Plant (Eds.), *Advances in experimental social psychology* (Vol. 47, pp. 1–53). Academic Press. https://doi.org/10.1016/B978-0-12-407236-7.00001-2

Given, M. (2023). *In defense of optimistic pessimism*. https://www.thecrimson.com/article/2023/1/27/matt-optimistic-pessimism/?cid=other-eml-mtg-mip-mck&hlkid=13f1ccf25eaa4678a9d2e58802285719&hctky=1926&hdpid=d16fd902-1a9a-476d-9a61-71983b7bedff

Goleman, D. (2020). *Emotional intelligence* (25th Anniversary edition). Bloomsbury.

Gruber, J., Hargittai, E., & Nguyen, M. H. (2022). The value of face-to-face communication in the digital world: What people miss about in-person interactions when those are limited. *Studies in Communication Sciences, 22*(3), 1–19. https://doi.org/10.24434/j.scoms.2022.03.3340

Harari, T. T., Sela, Y., Bareket-Bojmel, L. (2022, August). Gen Z during the COVID-19 crisis: A comparative analysis of the differences between Gen Z and Gen X in resilience, values and attitudes. *Current Psychology*. https://doi.org/10.1007/s12144-022-03501-4

Helliwell, J. F., Layard, R., & Sachs, J. D. (2019). World happiness report. https://worldhappiness.report/ed/2019/

Helliwell, J. F., Layard, R., Sachs, J. D., & De Neve, J. E. (2021). *World happiness report.* https://worldhappiness.report/ed/2021/

Herrman, H., Stewart, D. E., Diaz-Granados, N., Berger, E. L., Jackson, B., & Yuen, T. (2011). What is resilience? *The Canadian Journal of Psychiatry, 56*(5), 258–265. https://doi.org/10.1177/070674371105600504

Isen, A. M., & Geva, N. (1987). The influence of positive affect on acceptable level of risk: The person with a large canoe has a large worry. *Organizational Behavior and Human Decision Processes, 39*(2), 145–154.

Jacobs, S. (2022). Gen Z in Crisis: Blending EMDR and art therapy for a more robust therapeutic experience. In E. Davis, J. Fitzgerald, S. Jacobs, & J. Marchand (Eds.), *EMDR and creative arts therapies* (pp. 138–175). Routledge.

Johansen, B., & Euchner, J. (2013). Navigating the VUCA world. *Research-Technology Management, 56*(1), 10–15. https://doi.org/10.5437/08956308X5601003

Joshanloo, M. (2014). Eastern conceptualizations of happiness: Fundamental differences with western views. *Journal of Happiness Studies, 15,* 475–493. https://doi.org/10.1007/s10902-013-9431-1

Judge, T. A., & Kammeyer-Mueller, J. D. (2011). Happiness as a societal value. *Academy of Management Perspectives, 25*(1), 30–41.

Katzman, B., Dolev, N., & Koslowski, M. (2021). Social emotional support on one-on-one and group family WhatsApp. Do gender differences exist? *American Journal of Research in Medical Science, 6*(3), 1–3. https://doi.org/10.33425/2832-4226/21012

Kok, B. E., & Fredrickson, B. L (2010). Upward spirals of the heart: Autonomic flexibility, as indexed by vagal tone, reciprocally and prospectively predicts positive emotions and social connectedness. *Biological Psychology, 85*(3), 432–436.

Lower, K. E. (2014). *Understanding resilience and happiness among college students* (Doctoral dissertation). Middle Tennessee State University.

Machová, R., Zsigmond, T., & Lazanyl, K. (2020). Generations and emotional intelligence: A pilot study. *Acta Polytechnica Hungarica, 17,* 229–247. https://doi.org/10.12700/APH.17.5.2020.5.12

McKinsey Global Institute. (2017). *Jobs lost, jobs gained: Workplace transitions in the time of automation.* McKinsey and Company. https://www.mckinsey.com/~/media/mckinsey/industries/public%20and%20social%20sector/our%20insights/what%20the%20future%20of%20work%20will%20mean%20for%20jobs%20skills%20and%20wages/mgi%20jobs%20lost-jobs%20gained_report_december%202017.pdf

Modisane, K. T. (2023). The pursuit of happiness: Efforts of global leadership and followers to achieve social harmony. In S. Dihman, J. F. Marques, J. Schmieder-Ramirez, & P. G. Malakyan (Eds.), *Handbook of global leadership and followership* (chapter 31). Springer International Publishing.

Oishi, S., Graham, J., Kesebir, S., & Galinha, I. C. (2013). Concepts of happiness across time and cultures. *Personality and Social Psychology Bulletin, 39*(5), 559–577. https://doi.org/10.1016/j.adolescence.2016.12.008

Öztemel, K., & Yildiz-Akyol, E. (2021). The predictive role of happiness, social support, and future time orientation in career adaptability. *Journal of Career Development, 48*(3), 199–212.

Pew Research Center. (2018). *Smartphone ownership is growing rapidly around the world, but not always equally.* https://www.pewresearch.org/global/2019/02/05/smartphone-ownership-is-growing-rapidly-around-the-world-but-not-always-equally/

Reis, M., Matos, M. G., & Ramiro, L. (2019). Worries, mental and emotional health difficulties of Portuguese university students. *Advances in Social Sciences Research Journal, 6*(7), 558–569. https://doi.org/10.14738/assrj.67.6818

Reyes, M. E. S., Carmen, B. P. B., & Luminarias, M. E. P. (2021, July). An investigation into the relationship between climate change anxiety and mental health among Gen Z Filipinos. *Current Psychology.* https://doi.org/10.1007/s12144-021-02099-3

Ryan, R. M., & Deci, E. L. (2001). On happiness and human potentials: A review of research on hedonic and eudaimonic well-being. *Annual Review of Psychology, 52*(1), 141–166.

Ryff, C. D. (2008). Challenges and opportunities at the interface of aging, personality, and well-being. In O. P. John, R. W. Robins, & L. A. Pervin (Eds.), *Handbook of personality: Theory and research* (pp. 399–418). The Guilford Press.

Scorsolini-Comin, F., Fontaine, A. M. G. V., Koller, S. H., & Santos, M. A. D. (2013). From authentic happiness to well-being: The flourishing of positive psychology. *Psicologia: Reflexão e Crítica, 26*, 663–670.

Seemiller, C., & Grace, M. (2016). *Generation Z goes to College.* Jossey-Bass.

Seemiller, C., & Grace, M. (2019). *Generation Z: A century in the making.* Routledge.

Seligman, M. (2004). *Authentic happiness.* Simon & Schuster.

Seligman, M. (2011). *Flourish: A new understanding of happiness, well-being and how to achieve them.* Nicholas Brearley Publication.

Selye, H. (1976). Stress without Distress. In G. Serban (Ed.), *Psychopathology of human adaptation.* Springer. https://doi.org/10.1007/978-1-4684-2238-2_9

Sladek, S., & Grabinger, A. (2014). *Gen Z: The first generation of the 21st century has arrived.* https://www.xyzuniversity.com/wp-content/uploads/2018/08/GenZ_Final-dl1.pdf

Smaliukiene, R., & Bekesiene, S. (2020). Towards sustainable human resources: How generational differences impact subjective wellbeing in the military? *Sustainability, 12*(23), 10016. https://doi.org/10.3390/su122310016

SmartCitti. (n.d.). *The future of happiness: Gen Z in focus.* https://smartcitti.com/blog/template/the-future-of-happiness-generation-z-in-focus

Stein, S. J., & Book, H. E. (2011). *The EQ edge: Emotional intelligence and your success.* Jossey-Bass.

Veluchamy, R., Agrawal, V., & Krishnan, A. R. (2016). Perception on managing mental health of generation Z students in creating student superstars: Students' talent management. *International Journal of Pharmaceutical Sciences Review and Research, 39*(2), 45–52.

Waldinger, R. (2015, December). *What makes a good life? Lessons from the longest study on happiness* [Video]. TED Conferences. https://www.ted.com/talks/robert_waldinger_what_makes_a_good_life_lessons_from_the_longest_study_on_happiness/comments

Wani, M., & Dar, A. A. (2017). Optimism, happiness, and self-esteem among university students. *Indian Journal of Positive Psychology, 8*(3), 275–279.

Chapter 4

Communication Preferences and Behaviors

Shefaly Shorey[a], Daria Vyugina[b], Natalia Waechter[c] and Niva Dolev[d]

[a]National University of Singapore, Singapore
[b]Lomonosov Moscow State University, Russia
[c]University of Graz, Austria
[d]Kinneret College on the Sea of Galilee, Israel

Abstract

The rise of the digital era has greatly transformed communication, enabling it to transcend time and geographic boundaries. Generation Z grew up in this era and was exposed to a wide range of communication options, including in-app messaging, video calls, and social media platforms. Increased connectivity made possible by technological advancements has resulted in changes in communication etiquette and opened up more room for miscommunication. Despite heavily engaging in digital communication like text or in-app messaging, this generation still prefers to communicate face-to-face.

Keywords: Communication; social media; digital era; etiquette; connectivity; apps

The rise of the digital era has greatly transformed communication, enabling it to transcend time and geographical boundaries. Communication has evolved from face-to-face interactions and written correspondence to phone calls, emails, text messages, and video calls. By the time Gen Zers came of age and learned how to communicate, the wide range of digitally mediated communication options, including in-app messaging, video calls, and social media platforms, had become commonplace. This technological era is all they have ever known, shaping the way they view the world and, thus, communicate with others. Growing up in such an era, it is not surprising that those in Generation Z have developed communication styles and preferences that vary from those of previous generations.

Gen Z Around the World, 31–42
Copyright © 2024 Shefaly Shorey, Daria Vyugina, Natalia Waechter and Niva Dolev
Published under exclusive licence by Emerald Publishing Limited
doi:10.1108/978-1-83797-092-620241004

Evolving methods of communications have certain implications. For example, due to the availability of text messages, conversations with others no longer need to be continuous and synchronous. Exchanges between people can occur back and forth throughout the day without them having to be in the same space (Seemiller & Grace, 2019). Online communication via the internet also expands one's social circle, as it has become easier for individuals with similar interests to connect, even if they are from different parts of the world (Chan et al., 2020).

As internet penetration rates continue to grow around the world, it is not surprising that Gen Zers are more likely to engage in online modes of communication (Poushter et al., 2018). While people from high-income countries are more likely to own a smartphone, which makes it even easier for them to communicate on online platforms, those from low- and middle-income countries tend to communicate via Facebook and Twitter more than people from high-income countries (Poushter et al., 2018).

Communication Preferences

Reflecting back over the last several decades, many different types of communication modalities have emerged, often aligning with a particular generational cohort's coming of age. For example, despite being invented long before their birth, Baby Boomers grew up when the telephone was a primary source of communication; Gen Xers with email; Millennials with text messaging; and Gen Zers with social media messaging. New modalities don't take the place of old ones, per se; they simply become yet another way to communicate with one another.

In the Global Gen Z Study, Gen Zers were asked about their preferences among a variety of communication modalities – whether they "like to use this method," "somewhat like to use this method," or "do not like this method." The majority of Gen Zers like in-person conversation, followed by text messaging and direct messaging through an app. Far fewer like phone calls, video calls, or emails. Table 4.1 includes a breakdown of the percentage of Gen Zers who indicated liking each communication method.

The higher rates of preferences for in-person conversations may be due to Gen Zers wanting a sense of connection, rather than simply a mode for transferring information to one another. Seemiller and Grace (2019) shared a quote from a Gen Zer from their previous study that sums up this sentiment: "I usually prefer to talk in person with someone because you can better connect with whomever

Table 4.1. Preferences in Communication Methods.

Method	Like to Use This Method
In-person conversation	77%
Text messaging	54%
Direct messaging	47%
Telephone call	28%
Video chat	23%
Email messaging	17%

you are talking to. You can't read facial/body expressions through phone or email. Only with the human interaction."

Text messaging had the second highest preference rate, which is not surprising given that text messaging can serve various functions such as sending written text, photos, voice messages, or videos. In addition, expression elements like emojis, memes, and stickers contribute to the wide usage of text messages as a form of communication, as they make dialogues more interesting, humorous, vivid, and expressive (Fei et al., 2021).

Email messaging was the least preferred among all modalities. This finding aligns with other research that found that 67% of Gen Zers rarely or never use email (Claveria, 2021). Email stands in stark contrast to what is alluring about text and direct messaging – shorter bursts of communication with quicker response times along with the ability to easily include expression elements as well as share photos and videos.

In looking at communication preferences by region (Table 4.2), the results are similar to those at the global level. Aside from the Confucian and Africa regions, in-person conversation was the most preferred modality across regions. But, looking deeper with region, there may be differences by country. For example, research by Ari and Laron (2014) found Jewish youth prefer face-to-face inter-actions at greater rates than Arab youth. This might be attributed to language or cultural barriers. Gen Z Arab students are typically studying in Hebrew-speaking institutions and often feel alienated regarding their social, language, cultural, and religious conditions (Ari & Laron, 2014; Redlich, 2020), especially when face-to-face contacts are in a second language for them. Furthermore, Arab adolescents use their phones to stay connected with those in their local communities when face-to-face communication is not an option, or to discreetly communicate with the opposite gender so as to avoid violating social and cultural norms (Mesch & Talmud, 2008).

Messaging, in general, was the second most preferred modality in the Global Gen Z Study, albeit text messaging for the African-Islamic, English-speaking, Latin America, Protestant Europe, and West and South Asia regions and direct messaging through an app for the Orthodox Europe, Catholic Europe, and Africa regions. The Confucian region actually has direct messaging as their most preferred.

Consistent throughout the regions, similar to the global findings, email messaging was the least preferred communication modality.

However, preference reflects the extent someone likes to do something, whereas use reflects if, and to what extent, that person employs a specific modality. While Gen Zers may prefer a certain way of communicating in their personal time, their workplaces may require them to use modalities they have a lower preference for – like email for formal communication. Surprisingly, though, the rankings for preference and use were actually similar, as outlined in Table 4.3.

In-person conversation was the highest, and text messaging was the second highest. Interestingly, the *preferred* mode of communication corresponds to the *actual use* of communication methods only regarding the ranking, whereas the percentages for most modalities differed, above all for text messaging (69% actual

Table 4.2. Communication Modality Preferences Across Regions.

	In-Person Conversation	Text Messaging	Direct Messaging	Telephone Call	Video Chat	Email Messaging
Africa[a]	50%	65%	68%	56%	52%	32%
African-Islamic	76%	59%	54%	20%	25%	19%
Catholic Europe	84%	41%	48%	27%	25%	12%
Confucian	37%	16%	76%	29%	18%	12%
English-speaking	79%	58%	43%	26%	27%	21%
Latin America	76%	59%	54%	20%	25%	19%
Orthodox Europe	76%	57%	61%	34%	17%	16%
Protestant Europe	80%	63%	27%	24%	19%	23%
West and South Asia	74%	57%	36%	22%	28%	7%

[a]Not included in the World Values Survey.

Table 4.3. Communication Modality Use Across Regions.

Modality	Actual Use of This Modality	Like to Use This Modality
In-person conversation	79%	77%
Text messaging	69%	54%
Direct messaging	60%	47%
Telephone call	38%	28%
Video chat	25%	23%
Email messaging	21%	17%

use compared to 54% preferred), in-app messaging (60% actual use compared to 47% preferred), and telephone calls (38% actual use compared to 28% preferred). In contrast, the use of and preference for in-person conversation was similar (79% actual use compared to 77% preferred).

Use of particular communication modalities also differs somewhat across regions. See Table 4.4 for an overview.

For those regions whose highest preference ratings were for in-person conversation, all but two had their highest use rates for in-person conversation as well. The two outliers offered only slight differences. For example, Orthodox Europe had 78% for in-person conversation and 79% for direct messaging (which was the second most preferred), and Protestant Europe had 86% for in-person conversation and 90% for text messaging (which was also the second most preferred).

For most modalities, the use rate was higher than the preference rate across regions (i.e., English-speaking had 32% use rate for email messaging but only 21% preference for it). This indicates that many Gen Zers are engaging in communication methods they need but don't actually prefer. However, there does not appear to be a modality, generally that Gen Zers prefer more than they use, making it challenging to offer a suggestion for modality use.

Social Media

With a variety of social media platforms to choose from, Gen Zers clearly have their preferences. Table 4.5 includes the seven most frequently used platforms, of 14, from the Global Gen Z Study.

The platform most frequently used was Instagram, which mainly uses photos or videos to communicate ideas and serves as a space where many youth express themselves (Romero Saletti et al., 2022; Waechter, 2021). Pew Research Center found that 76% of 18- to 24-year-olds in the United States reported using Instagram, a rate much higher than their older counterparts; other than YouTube, it was the platform with the highest percentage of users (Auxier & Anderson,

Table 4.4. Communication Modality Use Across Regions.

	In-Person Conversation	Text Messaging	Direct Messaging	Telephone Call	Video Chat	Email Messaging
Africa	73%	88%	72%	68%	64%	25%
African-Islamic	68%	70%	47%	43%	23%	12%
Catholic Europe	87%	53%	64%	35%	21%	14%
Confucian	51%	10%	91%	35%	25%	6%
English-speaking	81%	76%	55%	36%	30%	32%
Latin America	73%	69%	67%	21%	30%	22%
Orthodox Europe	78%	69%	79%	54%	19%	17%
Protestant Europe	86%	90%	36%	28%	21%	24%
West and South Asia	61%	89%	54%	24%	48%	15%

[a]Not included in the World Values Survey.

Table 4.5. Most Frequently Used Communication Platform.

Platform	Most Frequently Used
Instagram	31%
WhatsApp	23%
YouTube	12%
Snapchat	12%
TikTok	9%
Facebook	6%
Twitter	4%

2021). A study of UK students pointed out the pros and cons of Instagram. On the one hand, it is useful for making and maintaining friendships; on the other, curated posts can showcase unattainable ideals, the need for connection and likes can result in an ongoing search for social acceptance, and cyberbullying can occur (Moreton & Greenfield, 2022).

WhatsApp garnered the next highest rate of frequency of use, primarily due to the global participant pool where WhatsApp is a key communication tool for messaging across countries and it fosters convenient and effective communication (Chan et al., 2020) and has had a positive impact on users' lives (Chan et al., 2020). Furthermore, WhatsApp is perceived as a platform for providing and receiving practical and emotional social support (Kaye & Quinn, 2020) by sharing life events in nearly real-time, giving and receiving advice, as well as creating a high sense of presence in communications (Karapanos et al., 2016).

When looking by region at the most frequently used social media platforms, the numbers tell a slightly different story. Table 4.6 showcases this variation.

While there are regional differences, it is interesting to see global overlap and similarities in the most frequently used platforms. Of note, the Confucian and Latin America regions gravitated toward Facebook, at 25% each, a higher number than other regions. While Instagram is the most frequently used platform among the aggregate global cohort, higher rates were found among Gen Zers in the Orthodox Europe (48%), African-Islamic (36%), and Catholic Europe (32%) regions. Gen Zers in the Protestant Europe (54%), Catholic Europe (42%), and African-Islamic (37%) regions noted WhatsApp as their most frequently used platform more than other regions. And while only 12% of the global Gen Z cohort indicated Snapchat as their most frequently used platform, nearly one in three (29%) of the Gen Zers in the English-speaking region report Snapchat as their most cited platform of use.

Communication apps, though, can serve different purposes. In the Global Gen Z Study, participants were asked how they use each of the 14 platforms. Participants reported using Instagram (62%), WhatsApp (42%), and Snapchat (36%) for keeping up with others. For sharing personal information, they reported using

Table 4.6. Most Frequently Used Communication Platform by Region.

	Instagram	WhatsApp	YouTube	Snapchat	TikTok	Facebook	Twitter
Africa[a]	0%	63%	4%	0%	7%	22%	4%
African-Islamic	36%	37%	8%	3%	5%	3%	5%
Catholic Europe	32%	42%	11%	3%	6%	1%	3%
Confucian	13%	13%	0%	0%	0%	25%	0%
English-speaking	25%	5%	15%	29%	16%	2%	4%
Latin America	21%	29%	9%	0%	6%	25%	8%
Orthodox Europe	48%	11%	14%	3%	5%	14%	1%
Protestant Europe	18%	54%	8%	3%	11%	0%	1%
West and South Asia	26%	17%	11%	0%	9%	7%	0%

[a]Not included in the World Values Survey.

WhatsApp (46%), Instagram (45%), and Snapchat (27%). These three apps appear to be the most prominent for Gen Zers when connecting and communicating with others.

For learning and obtaining new knowledge, Gen Zers gravitate toward YouTube (72%), Instagram (42%), and WhatsApp (33%), all which share video features. While 31% use WhatsApp to share their own expertise, content, or opinions, which is similar to the number who use the platform for learning, only 10% use YouTube, and 18% use Instagram.

As a global cohort, it appears Generation Z uses Instagram and WhatsApp for multiple purposes (i.e., sharing about themselves, sharing their opinions/expertise, and keeping up with others) but have a more distinct intention in using Snapchat mostly for following others and posting about their lives as well as YouTube primarily for learning.

Challenges with Social Media

Managing various modes of social media communication can lead to various challenges for members of Generation Z, including issues around miscommunication, self-worth, social skills, limited worldviews, and scammers.

Miscommunication

It has also been found that the use of abbreviations, lack of punctuation, and internet slang hurt the writing skills of Generation Z, which can have an impact on their ability to communicate properly in formal settings (Half, 2015; Iorgulescu, 2016). Furthermore, spell checks and "auto-correct" can affect their language skills as they become dependent on the language system in devices to correct their mistakes (Akram & Kumar, 2017). In addition, the use of internet lingo in daily life can affect Gen Zers' communication with individuals from other generations who are unfamiliar with these new ways of speech (Grabe, 2011). Without a common understanding of a word, the intended meaning may be misinterpreted and the conversation can become awkward or uncomfortable.

In addition to misunderstandings in the messaging, responding to different people on the same platform can increase the likelihood of accidentally sending a response to the wrong person (Seemiller & Grace, 2019). Such miscommunication can also occur when individuals are unable to convey their intended meanings accurately due to the absence of nonverbal cues like body language and facial expressions (Kurniasih, 2017). Furthermore, some studies (Agarwal & Lu, 2020; Hoyle et al., 2017) have found that not replying to messages from others can lead to misunderstandings. The "seen by" and "last seen" features contribute to such misunderstandings, as senders might feel that they are ignoring their message on purpose (Hoyle et al., 2017).

Self-Worth

As they tend to communicate via text messages frequently from a young age (Richards et al., 2015), Gen Zers might have tied their sense of self-worth partially to being responded to (Agarwal & Lu, 2020). Thus, they start to overthink why their friends or family members are not responding to their messages, which can affect their relationships and mood.

Social Skills

While social media can facilitate the formation of offline friendships, which may help reduce loneliness, some Gen Zers may feel that making friends online is much easier than doing so in real life, which can lead them to engage in more online communication rather than socialize in person (Allen et al., 2014).

Gen Zers' social skills then may be affected if they tend to communicate almost exclusively on online platforms and lack sufficient physical communication opportunities. Lacking ample experience with face-to-face communication may affect their ability to read nonverbal cues and to maintain eye contact, which operates the mirror neurons that underlie empathy (Iacoboni, 2009).

Limited Worldviews

Furthermore, due to the wide accessibility of information via technology and social media, Gen Zers can also easily find people with similar perspectives, decreasing the possibility of expanding their worldviews and developing empathy (Manney, 2008).

Scammers

As people can create false identities online, Gen Zers might fall victim to scams, phishing attacks, or other dangers if they are not properly educated on the risks that come with befriending others on the internet (Fire et al., 2014; Kurniasih, 2017). They might not be aware of the other party's identity, as it can be easy for scammers or predators to conceal their actual persona. Their social media accounts may also be hijacked, causing them to lose the online connections that they had with their loved ones. Young people are often a target of online threats, especially online predators who seek to sexually or financially exploit younger and more vulnerable children and teenagers (Fire et al., 2014). A recent study shows that the majority of young people reported having been exposed to harmful content, cyber hate, and sexting online (Waechter et al., 2021).

Conclusion

Changes in communication over the years have allowed those in Generation Z to familiarize themselves with different modes of communication and to interact and exchange ideas with people from around the world. The results from the Global Gen Z study show that despite the overall preference for face-to-face communication, Generation Z also prefers to engage in online communication. However, there are still some pitfalls and risks to the more recent modes of communication, such as miscommunication due to having many ongoing chats, having poorer writing skills, craving the opportunity to develop social skills through in-person interaction, and being the target of online fraud and violence. Therefore, it is important to ensure that Gen Zers recognize the usefulness and risks of various communication modalities and focus on developing skills that could have become less developed but are particularly relevant regarding the time spent engaging in digital communication.

As it is very common for individuals to use online platforms to meet others from different cultural backgrounds, cultural literacy is important. Therefore, Generation Z individuals need knowledge on other cultures to avoid inadvertently engaging in disrespectful behavior.

Along with changes in communication, etiquette changes have also occurred (Seemiller & Grace, 2019). In engaging in online platforms, Generation Z is aware of the different forms of appropriate etiquette (Dewi et al., 2021). However, it is still critical to spend time helping those in Generation Z learn and develop the skills to awareness to engage effectively and appropriately with others, in person or online.

References

Agarwal, N. K., & Lu, W. (2020). Response to non-response: How people react when their smartphone messages and calls are ignored. *Proceedings of the Association for Information Science and Technology, 57*(1), 1–14.

Akram, W., & Kumar, R. (2017). A study on positive and negative effects of social media on society. *International Journal of Computer Sciences and Engineering, 5*(10), 351–354.

Allen, K. A., Ryan, T., Gray, D. L., McInerney, D. M., & Waters, L. (2014). Social media use and social connectedness in adolescents: The positives and the potential pitfalls. *The Educational and Developmental Psychologist, 31*(1), 18–31.

Ari, L. L., & Laron, D. (2014). Intercultural learning in graduate studies at an Israeli college of education: Attitudes toward multiculturalism among Jewish and Arab students. *Higher Education, 68*(2), 243–262.

Auxier, B., & Anderson, M. (2021). *Social media use in 2021.* https://www.pewresearch.org/internet/2021/04/07/social-media-use-in-2021/

Chan, T. J., Yong, W. K., & Harmizi, A. (2020). Usage of WhatsApp and interpersonal communication skills among private university students. *Journal of Arts and Social Sciences, 3*(2), 15–25.

Claveria, K. (2021). *Study: Gen Zs and Millennials are ignoring emails, putting the future of market research at risk.* https://www.rivaltech.com/blog/gen-z-millennials-ignoring-email-surveys

Dewi, C., Pahriah, P., & Purmadi, A. (2021). The urgency of digital literacy for generation Z students in chemistry learning. *International Journal of Emerging Technologies in Learning (IJET), 16*(11), 88–103.

Fei, Z., Li, Z., Zhang, J., Feng, Y., & Zhou, J. (2021). *Towards expressive communication with internet memes: A new multimodal conversation dataset and benchmark.* arXiv preprint arXiv:2109.01839.

Fire, M., Goldschmidt, R., & Elovici, Y. (2014). Online social networks: Threats and solutions. *IEEE Communications Surveys & Tutorials, 16*(4), 2019–2036.

Grabe, E. (2011). e-English: A natural evolution of our language? *City Tech Article, 6*, 28–31.

Half, R. (2015). *Get ready for Generation Z.* roberthalf.com

Hoyle, R., Das, S., Kapadia, A., Lee, A. J., & Vaniea, K. (2017). *Was my message read? Privacy and signaling on Facebook Messenger.* In *Proceedings of the 2017 CHI Conference on Human Factors in Computing Systems.*

Iacoboni, M. (2009). Imitation, empathy, and mirror neurons. *Annual Review of Psychology, 60*, 653–670. https://doi.org/10.1146/annurev.psych.60.110707.163604

Iorgulescu, M.-C. (2016). Generation Z and its perception of work. *Cross-Cultural Management Journal, 18*(1), 319–325.

Karapanos, E., Teixeira, P., & Gouveia, R. (2016). Need fulfillment and experiences on social media: A case on Facebook and WhatsApp. *Computers in Human Behavior, 55*, 888–897.

Kaye, L. K., & Quinn, S. (2020). Psychosocial outcomes associated with engagement with online chat systems. *International Journal of Human-Computer Interaction, 36*(2), 190–198.

Kurniasih, N. (2017). Paralinguistics cues used and miscommunication on social media: Case study of students of Communication Science Program. In *The 1st International Conference on Language, Linguistics in Literature* (pp. 319–325).

Manney, P. J. (2008). Empathy in the time of technology: How storytelling is the key to empathy. *Journal of Evolution and Technology, 19*(1), 51–61.

Mesch, G., & Talmud, I. (2008). Cultural differences in communication technology use: Adolescent Jews and Arabs in Israel. In J. E. Katz (Ed.), *Handbook of mobile communication studies* (pp. 313–324). The MIT Press.

Moreton, L., & Greenfield, S. (2022). University students' views on the impact of Instagram on mental wellbeing: A qualitative study. *BMC Psychology, 10*(45), 1–10. https://doi.org/10.1186/s40359-022-00743-6

Poushter, J., Bishop, C., & Chwe, H. (2018). Social media use continues to rise in developing countries but plateaus across developed ones. https://www.pewresearch.org/global/2018/06/19/social-media-use-continues-to-rise-in-developing-countries-but-plateaus-across-developed-ones/

Redlich, O. (2020). Intercultural competence among Jewish and Arab students studying together in an academic institution in Israel. *World Academy of Science, Engineering and Technology International Journal of Educational and Pedagogical Sciences, 14*(7), 508–515.

Richards, D., Caldwell, P. H., & Go, H. (2015). Impact of social media on the health of children and young people. *Journal of Paediatrics and Child Health, 51*(12), 1152–1157.

Romero Saletti, S. M., Van den Broucke, S., & Van Beggelaer, W. (2022). Understanding motives, usage patterns and effects of Instagram use in youths: A qualitative study. *Emerging Adulthood, 10*(6), 1376–1394. https://doi.org/10.1177/21676968221114251

Seemiller, C., & Grace, M. (2019). *Generation Z: A century in the making.* Routledge.

Waechter, N. (2021). Gendered social media cultures between individuality and collectivity in adolescence. In V. Cuzzocrea, B. Gook, & B. Schiermer (Eds.), *Forms of collectivity among contemporary youth: A global perspective* (pp. 185–206). Brill.

Waechter, N., Stuhlpfarrer, E., Böttcher, C., Bernhardt, M., & Kadera, S. (2021). *Digital skills of young people.* Results of the ySKILLS Survey Wave 1 (2021). National Report Germany. ySKILLS.

Chapter 5

Developing and Fostering Relationships

Gudrun Quenzel[a], Francesca Beretta[b], Niva Dolev[c],
Natalia Waechter[d], Stepanka Kadera[e], Mariya Karaivanova[f]
and Radka Massaldjieva[f]

[a]University of Education of Vorarlberg, Austria
[b]University of Kansas, USA
[c]Kinneret College on the Sea of Galilee, Israel
[d]University of Graz, Austria
[e]Ludwig Maximilian University of Munich, Germany
[f]Medical University of Plovdiv, Bulgaria

Abstract

Having good relationships with friends and a trusting romantic partnership are extremely important for members of Generation Z. In social relationships with other young people, they experience solidarity and support with problems and crises, and learn to stand by others. Young people are therefore intensely concerned with how to enter into relationships and their expectations of them. Overwhelmingly, what they are looking for in friendships is similar across cultures – a set of shared values and similar hobbies. For romantic relationships, though, shared values and close proximity are key.

Keywords: Social relations; friends; romantic relationships; values; hobbies; interests

Forming interpersonal relationships with peers and significant others is one of the main developmental tasks of adolescents and those entering early adulthood (Erikson, 1968). Thus, in the transition from childhood to adolescence, young people's peer groups grow in importance (Hojjat & Moyer, 2017; Wendt, 2019), and their networks get more extensive. However, not only do the quantity of friendships and relationships increase, but also the quality of these relationships (Way & Greene, 2006).

Gen Z Around the World, 43–51
Copyright © 2024 Gudrun Quenzel, Francesca Beretta, Niva Dolev, Natalia Waechter, Stepanka Kadera, Mariya Karaivanova and Radka Massaldjieva
Published under exclusive licence by Emerald Publishing Limited
doi:10.1108/978-1-83797-092-620241005

Against the backdrop of an increasingly individualized world and a decline in socially binding norms (Beck & Beck-Gernsheim, 2002; Howard, 2019), it is critical to understand what friendships and romantic partnerships look like for Generation Z and the factors that are important to them when entering these relationships.

Friendships

Friendship plays an important role in the formation of social competence (Newcomb & Bagwell, 1995; Rubin et al., 2007) and self-esteem development (Hartup & Stevens, 1999) as well as prepares young people for the successful management of the future demands of adult romantic life (Allen et al., 2020). The developmental functions of friendships include testing intimacy, negotiating gender identity, supporting detachment from parents, preparing for partnerships, resolving conflicts, learning to recognize and understand the feelings of others, and learn to stand by others. Thus, in trusting relationships with others, young people can experience solidarity and support in problems and crises. Therefore, friendship becomes a protective factor in situations of social and emotional troubles (Ciairano et al., 2007; Scholte & van Aken, 2020). Not surprisingly, quality friendships also increase young peoples' well-being (Hartup & Stevens, 1999).

In addition to the developmental benefits of friendship, having good relationships with friends is also extremely important for members of Generation Z (Scholte & van Aken, 2020; Wolfert & Quenzel, 2019). During the pandemic, however, friendship-making shifted for many Gen Zers as they felt more isolated, particularly those who were starting new jobs, had moved to new cities, or were beginning their studies at a new school (Klein & Noenickx, 2023). This led to greater efforts on their parts to either connect with old friends or to flock online to friendship apps (Klein & Noenickx, 2023).

Despite their nuanced way of developing and fostering friendships, most Gen Zers are fairly clear about what they look for in their friends. In the Global Gen Z Study, participants were asked to rate seven possible factors on their level of importance in making new friends. Table 5.1 outlines the percentage of participants who indicated that the specified factor was important or very important.

Table 5.1. Factors in Making New Friends.

	Very Important or Important
Having similar values	73%
Having similar hobbies	42%
Being in close proximity to each other	30%
Having similar political viewpoints	24%
Having a shared culture or background	15%
Being affiliated with a particular group or organization	12%
Physical appearance	6%

Seventy-three percent of participants reported that it is important or very important that their friends share similar values, which aligns with previous empirical findings (e.g., Brown & Larson, 2009). Having similar values is not just about sharing the same worldviews, but values are shaped by social influences (Rokeach, 1973) and socialization processes (Bilsky & Schwartz, 1994), which may be similar with both individuals, highlighting a sense of familiarity or compatibility with each other.

Further, 42% indicated that shared hobbies are important or very important to them when making new friends, which makes sense in that friends usually come together to engage in specific activities like sports, clubs, hobbies, or just general interests. For almost a third of young people (30%), being in close proximity to their friends is important, although its lower percentage may be driven by the ability to connect with others across distance via digital technology and social media.

Given Generation Z's self-ascribed characteristic of open-mindedness as reported in the Global Gen Z Study, it's not surprising that only 15% think it is important to have a shared culture or background. Physical appearance is even less important to them with only six percent considering it as important in forming a friendship. It seems that many Gen Zers do not care so much about where their friends come from but instead want to connect with those who share their values.

In looking at factors important in developing a friendship, Gen Zers appear to be far more similar across World Values Regions (World Values Survey Association, 2022) than they are different. Table 5.2 showcases the percentage of participants from each region who indicated the specified factor was important or very important.

Having similar values is rated as the most important factor in all regions. There is some slight variation in the prevalence of this importance between the regions though. For instance, 88% of Gen Zers from Protestant Europe indicated shared values were important in new friendships whereas 55% of those in African-Islamic countries felt similarly. All other regions shared a similar prominence in which between 70 and 80% of Gen Zers believe shared values is an important factor in friendships. It is clear – sharing values with friends is the key to forming a good friendship.

For all but two regions, the next most important factor is having similar hobbies. However, the Gen Zers in the Protestant Europe and Confucian regions rated shared political viewpoints as the second most important factor in friendships, although similar hobbies was also highly rated for both regions.

In the end, physical appearance was reported as the least important factor in friendships for all regions. The Confucian region had the highest percentage of Gen Zers who indicated physical appearance matters in friendship, but with only 11%. Further, shared culture or background was not rated by many in Generation Z as an important factor; the highest rates include Latin America, the Confucian region, and West and South Asia at 30%, 29%, and 28%, respectively, with the lowest being in Protestant Europe (5%), Catholic Europe (9%), and English-Speaking (10%) regions.

Table 5.2. Important Factors in New Friendships by Region.

	Having Similar Values	Having Similar Hobbies	Close Proximity	Shared Political Viewpoints	Shared Culture or Background	Affiliation With a Group/Organization	Physical Appearance
Africa[a]	64%	35%	12%	16%	24%	12%	16%
African-Islamic	55%	37%	30%	15%	23%	18%	9%
Catholic Europe	80%	40%	27%	21%	9%	7%	4%
Confucian	75%	45%	37%	49%	29%	20%	11%
English-Speaking	74%	47%	38%	28%	10%	11%	5%
Latin America	77%	45%	22%	33%	30%	15%	7%
Orthodox Europe	70%	46%	23%	11%	19%	13%	6%
Protestant Europe	88%	24%	31%	38%	5%	5%	3%
West and South Asia	81%	35%	24%	4%	28%	9%	4%

[a]Not included in the World Values Survey.

It may be that the more individualistically oriented a society is, the less important a common cultural origin is in friendships.

Other than the Confucian and Protestant Europe regions who rated shared political viewpoints in their top three (replacing similar hobbies for Protestant Europe and close proximity for the Confucian region), all other regions had the highest percentages of importance for the same three factors – similar values, similar hobbies, and close proximity.

Romantic Relationships

Romantic relationships are often entered into for the first time in adolescence. Today, however, in many countries – and especially among young people with a university education – there are often many years between the first romantic ties in young adolescence and entering into a long-term emotional relationship, such as marriage or starting a family of one's own. For many young people, marriage and family are still highly desirable goals and they use these years to test out which form of relationship and which partner suits them (Murray & Arnett, 2019), whether that relationship is simply a friendship, committed relationship, or even a situationship, in which the connection is not entirely defined but can range from entirely casual to one that looks similar to a traditional relationship but without the expectations of a future together (Noenickx, 2022).

In addition to many taking time before settling on an actual life partner, Gen Zers are breaking other norms when it comes to dating (Brunson, 2023). For one, many in Generation Z are less trusting, particularly about being lured in by misleading dating profiles or fake photos (Cox, 2023). This hesitance is pulling many of them off the dating apps (Tolentino, 2023). Given only 19% of those in the Global Gen Z Study agreed with the statement, "I believe people are inherently good," it makes sense that many of them have skepticism and mistrust around online dating.

While only 29% are on the dating sites, a good number of them are still using digital means to connect with potential relationship partners, with their virtual space of choice being Instagram (Tolentino, 2023). Being able to direct message someone they see online holds less expectation that the outreach is intended to be romantic, which takes the pressure off both parties. This way, they can start as friends and see if there is a romantic spark that builds later on.

Many Gen Zers find these possible connections through their established friends list online, which not only makes meeting people easier but also ensures more vetting than if outreaching to a complete stranger. And, by being connected through social media, it is easy to scroll through someone's profile and get a fuller and possibly more accurate portrayal of their life than one would by looking at a dating profile.

This friend to partner trend seems to be a significant path for many Gen Zers (Brunson, 2023). A study by Business Insider found that while only 21% of those in older generations indicated that their spouse or partner was a friend first, 42% of young people noted that was the case (Cox, 2023). Gen Zers are drawn to friends as their romantic options because there is less uncertainty about the person than if they were to meet on a dating app (Cox, 2023). It makes sense then that what Gen Zers seek in romantic relationships looks remarkably similar to what they look for in friendships. Table 5.3 highlights important factors for Gen Zers in entering into romantic relationship.

Around the globe, having similar values is most important to young people when entering into a romantic partnership (80%), which has an even higher rate than what they reported for friendships (73%). For most, it is also very important to live or work nearby (58%), which confirms that the old-fashioned way of dating is not so old after all. Having the same hobbies is also important to some (44%). While a mismatch in political ideology may not necessarily be a determining factor in making new friends (24%), agreement on politics becomes a more sensitive matter when it comes to romance as 38% of Generation Z participants consider similar political viewpoints as important when entering a romantic relationship. Physical attributes are not a determining factor in the emotional development of a friendship (6%). However, appearance and looks matter to more Gen Zers in the development of a romantic relationship with 35% stating appearance is an important factor when entering into a partnership. But, what's most important for Gen Zers is sharing the same values, being in close proximity, having common interests, and for some, possessing the same political beliefs.

There are some differences between the regions, though, when it comes to important factors in romantic relationships, as outlined in Table 5.4.

While similar values are particularly important to young people in all regions, Gen Zers from Protestant Europe (92%), West and South Asia (91%), English-Speaking countries (85%), and Catholic Europe (84%) rate similar values particularly high in terms of importance.

After similar values, the second most important factor fluctuates between shared hobbies and close proximity. Shared hobbies is the second most important factor in romantic relationships for Gen Zers in the Confucian countries (59%) and West and South Asia (53%). Close proximity is ranked second in importance

Table 5.3. Factors When Entering Into a Romantic Relationships.

	Important or Very Important
Having similar values	80%
Being in close proximity to each other	58%
Having similar political viewpoints	38%
Having similar hobbies	44%
Physical appearance	35%
Having a shared culture or background	24%
Being affiliated with a particular group or organization	12%

Table 5.4. Important Factors in Romantic Relationships by Region.

	Having Similar Values	Having Similar Hobbies	Close Proximity	Shared Political Viewpoints	Shared Culture or Background	Affiliation With a Group/Organization	Physical Appearance
Africa[a]	76%	45%	64%	28%	30%	30%	14%
African-Islamic	65%	38%	44%	24%	36%	16%	35%
Catholic Europe	84%	43%	59%	34%	15%	6%	31%
Confucian	78%	59%	43%	56%	36%	19%	34%
English-Speaking	85%	48%	69%	47%	15%	11%	35%
Latin America	81%	49%	51%	44%	38%	17%	29%
Orthodox Europe	77%	46%	48%	18%	31%	14%	39%
Protestant Europe	92%	27%	69%	55%	12%	6%	33%
West and South Asia	91%	53%	44%	31%	32%	11%	26%

[a]Not included in the World Values Survey.

for those in Protestant Europe (69%), English-Speaking countries (69%), Africa (64%), Catholic Europe (59%), Latin America (51%), Orthodox Europe (48%), and African-Islamic countries (44%).

Those in the Confucian countries (56%) and Protestant Europe (55%) rate the political viewpoints of their partner higher than other regions. And, having a similar culture was more important to young people in the Latin America (38%), Confucian (36%), and African-Islamic regions (36%) but less important to the individualistic-oriented countries in Protestant Europe (12%), Catholic Europe (15%), and the English-Speaking countries (15%).

What Gen Zers seek in romantic relationships is remarkably similar to what they seek in friendships. Again, other than Confucian and Protestant Europe who rated shared political viewpoints in their top three (rather than shared hobbies for Protestant Europe and close proximity for the Confucian region), all other regions had the highest percentages of importance for similar values, similar hobbies, and close proximity for romantic relationships.

Conclusion

As it is with every young generation, making new friends and dating can be intimidating. However, this generation has come of age during a socially isolating pandemic, where their loneliness and somewhat mistrust of others has propelled them back into the comfort of existing connections and the online world, which some may find solace in. While parents, supervisors, and other trusted adults might have the best intentions of urging young people to strike up conversation with a stranger, put themselves out there, and just make new friends, it might not be that easy for many in Generation Z. Instead, helping to build their conversation and social skills as well as confidence for when they choose to reach out to new potential friends or romantic partners can be critical. Further, though, perhaps older generations can learn more about friendships and dating by making connections through friendship apps or embracing the friends first approach to dating that many Gen Zers use. Then, perhaps a Gen Zer will strike up a conversation at the grocery store with their potential love interest while their Gen Xer parent makes a new friend online.

What Gen Zers look for in both their friendships and relationships appears to be similar to each other and similar across global regions. For this generation worldwide, it matters less where people come from, what they do, and what they look like, and more so what matters to them.

References

Allen, J. P., Narr, R. K., Kansky, J., & Szwedo, D. E. (2020). Adolescent peer relationship qualities as predictors of long-term romantic life satisfaction. *Child Development, 91*(1), 327–340.

Beck, U., & Beck-Gernsheim, E. (2002). *Individualization: Institutionalized individualism and its social and political consequences.* SAGE.

Bilsky, W., & Schwartz, S. H. (1994). Values and personality. *European Journal of Personality, 8*, 163–181.

Brown, B. B., & Larson, J. (2009). Peer relationships in adolescence. In R. Lerner & L. Steinberg (Eds.), *Handbook of adolescent psychology: Contextual influences on adolescent development* (pp. 74–103). Wiley.

Brunson, P. C. (2023). *The future of dating 2023*. https://www.tinderpressroom.com/2023-05-22-welcome-to-a-renaissance-in-dating,-driven-by-authenticity

Ciairano, S., Rabaglietti, E., Roggero, A., Bonino, S., & Beyers, W. (2007). Patterns of adolescent friendships, psychological adjustment and antisocial behavior. *International Journal of Behavioral Development, 31*(6), 539–548.

Cox, D. (2023). *Gen Z's dating revolution*. https://www.businessinsider.com/gen-z-dating-trend-online-apps-friends-romantic-partners-relationships-2023-3

Erikson, E. H. (1968). *Identity, youth and crisis*. W. W. Norton Company.

Hartup, W. W., & Stevens, N. (1999). Friendships and adaptation across the life span. *Current Directions in Psychological Science, 8*(3), 76–79.

Hojjat, M., & Moyer, A. (Eds.). (2017). *The psychology of friendship*. University Press.

Howard, C. (2019). Individualization. In A. Elliott (Ed.), *Routledge handbook of identity studies* (pp. 130–146). Routledge.

Klein, J., & Noenickx, C. (2023). *Can Gen Z make friends in the pandemic era?* https://www.bbc.com/worklife/article/20230201-can-gen-z-make-friends-in-the-pandemic-era

Murray, J. L., & Arnett, J. J. (2019). *Emerging adulthood and higher education. A new student development paradigm*. Routledge.

Newcomb, A., & Bagwell, C. (1995). Children's friendship relations: A meta-analytic review. *Psychological Bulletin, 117*, 306–347.

Noenickx, C. (2022). *'Situationships:' Why Gen Z are embracing the grey area*. https://www.bbc.com/worklife/article/20220831-situationships-why-gen-z-are-embracing-the-grey-area

Rokeach, M. (1973). *The nature of human values*. Free Press.

Rubin, K., Bowker, J., & Oh, W. (2007). The peer relationships and friendships of socially withdrawn children. In A. S. LoCoco, K. H. Rubin, & C. Zappulla (Eds.), *L'isolamento sociale durante l'infanzia [Social withdrawal in childhood]*. Unicopli.

Scholte, R. H., & van Aken, M. A. (2020). Peer relations in adolescence. In S. Jackson & L. Goossens (Eds.), *Handbook of adolescent development* (pp. 175–199). Psychology Press.

Tolentino, D. (2023). *Gen Zers want to date more 'organically.' Some say Instagram brings them closer to that goal*. https://www.nbcnews.com/news/gen-z-organic-dating-instagram-rcna70459

Way, N., & Greene, M. L. (2006). Trajectories of perceived friendship quality during adolescence: The patterns and contextual predictors. *Journal of Research on Adolescence, 16*(2), 293–320.

Wendt, E. V. (2019). *Die Jugendlichen und ihr Umgang mit Sexualität, Liebe und Partnerschaft*. Kohlhammer.

Wolfert, S., & Quenzel, G. (2019). Vielfalt jugendlicher Lebenswelten: Familie, Partnerschaft, Religion und Freundschaft. In M. Albert, K. Hurrelmann, & G. Quenzel, Kantar (Hrsg.), *Jugend 2019* (pp. 133–161). Beltz.

World Values Survey Association. (2022). *World values survey*. https://www.worldvaluessurvey.org/WVSContents.jsp

Chapter 6

Family Dynamics

Shefaly Shorey[a], *Gonzalo Aza Blanc*[b], *Isabel Muñoz-San Roque*[b] *and Marta Hernández Arriaza*[b]

[a]National University of Singapore, Singapore
[b]Pontifical Comillas University, Spain

Abstract

Gen Zers are immensely family-oriented, valuing the connections they have with their parents and siblings. Growing up, Gen Zers were often supervised by their caregivers and grew up becoming more reliant on the attachment figures in their lives. In turn, they often have significant influence on their families, especially in terms of finance- and education-related decision-making. This can be attributed to the tech-savvy nature that enables them to efficiently seek out information online. Overall, Generation Z values having a loving family, and many desire a fulfilling life with a partner and children.

Keywords: Family dynamics; relationships; parenting; family influence; households; connection

Given the role they often play, family members often influence the mindsets, values, and decision-making processes of a generational cohort. And, this influence is no different among those in Generation Z. Prior global research (Broadbent et al., 2017) has found that having positive relationships with family members is a significant contributor to the happiness of Gen Zers.

Changing Perceptions of Families

Changes in parenting styles, values, and beliefs have led to the evolution of family dynamics for Generation Z, particularly in domestic chores, caregiving, multi-generational households, and divorce.

Gen Z Around the World, 53–59

Copyright © 2024 Shefaly Shorey, Gonzalo Aza Blanc, Isabel Muñoz-San Roque and Marta Hernández Arriaza

Published under exclusive licence by Emerald Publishing Limited

doi:10.1108/978-1-83797-092-620241006

Domestic Chores

Schneider et al. (2021) explained that for heterosexual couples, structural factors like working hours and the number of children were predictors of the division of household labor. This did not apply to same-sex couples, who subscribed more to egalitarian ideals (Schneider et al., 2021). When it comes to domestic chores, same-sex couples are found to have distributed the housework more equally than their heterosexual counterparts (Schneider et al., 2021). It is possible that heteronormative family values and ideals have a stronger influence on heterosexual couples than same-sex couples, although the trends observed in this generation have shown a movement toward more egalitarian ideals. With the continued acceptance and legalization of same-sex marriage in many countries around the world (Council on Foreign Relations, 2022), children growing up in these households may more readily experience this egalitarianism.

Caregiving

Despite the rise of maternal employment over the past few decades, mothers still hold more responsibility for childcare and other household duties, although fathers have gradually taken on more of the household workload (Craig & Mullan, 2011). Fathers are also more involved in the child-rearing of their Generation Z children compared to parents of kids from preceding generations (Huerta et al., 2014). This greater role for fathers aligns with the rise in the more recent rise in paternity leave for men (Kuo et al., 2018; Tamm, 2019). Thus, it isn't surprising that Generation Z preteen children with good relationships with their fathers have been found to have higher self-esteem, fewer injuries, and fewer behavioral problems (Oerther & Oerther, 2021).

Further, many Generation Z children grew up with high-levels of adult involvement, becoming reliant on these attachment figures in their lives (Malone, 2007). But, rather than these adults being "helicopter parents," where they hover over their children's every move, parents of Gen Zers are more similar to "co-pilots," where they play more of a coaching and mentoring role (Seemiller & Grace, 2019). This type of support is critical in that Gen Zers' perception of parental and family support has been found to contribute to the life satisfaction and psychosocial well-being of Generation Z adolescents (Oberle et al., 2011).

Multigenerational Households

With declining birth rates across the globe (Alvarez, 2023) and people having fewer children than they did in the past (Skirbekk, 2022), most Gen Zers have grown up in smaller households than kids from preceding generations. Despite some having fewer siblings, many Gen Zers have lived in multigenerational households in which more than two (i.e., parent/guardian and child) generations live in the same residence.

Multigenerational households allow for greater kin support and are often more common among fragile families (Pilkauskas, 2012). The global increase in multigenerational households aligns with the increase in dual-income families (OCSE, 2011), which then involves grandparents taking on the role of caretaker for many Generation Z children. A multigenerational household structure appears to be more present in households with young mothers or first-time parents, who may require more support and guidance in child-rearing (Pilkauskas, 2012). Grandparents may also serve as providers of stability for grandchildren during family crises, such as divorce or separation, incarceration, or the death of a parent (Goodman, 2007; Masfety et al., 2019). Hence, multigenerational households may have offered Gen Zers a larger support system growing up, possibly contributing to their family-oriented spirit.

In recent years, the number of children around the globe raised in three-generation households has increased significantly, especially in some English-speaking countries (Goodman, 2007; Masfety et al., 2019) and in Africa (Hall & Mokomane, 2018). Conversely, three-generation households in some Confucian as well as West and South Asian countries, like Japan and Singapore, have been on the decline (Lin, 2021; Miyazaki, 2021). Nonetheless, the proportion of multigenerational households remains high among these nations.

Divorce

Another characteristic of Generation Z is that many tend to hold an accepting view of the topic of divorce (Sumari et al., 2020). In such circumstances, Gen Zers still wish to maintain a good connection with both parents, often claiming that the divorce "was their parents' choice and they did not wish to question their decision" (Sumari et al., 2020, p. 201). This can also be an attempt for them to stay out of the parental conflict and continue having a positive relationship with their parents. Sumari et al. (2020) found that while many adolescents were shocked by the dissolving of their parent's marriage, they ultimately adapted well because they were able to receive counseling, which may have contributed to their openness to tending to their mental well-being, in general (Seemiller & Grace, 2019).

Collaborative Decision-Making

Parents and family members of Gen Zers play a large role in impacting this cohort's behaviors, particularly when it comes to decision-making. Based on findings from the Global Gen Z Study, a large proportion of the Gen Zers reported that their family members greatly influence their decision-making. Table 6.1 outlines the three family groupings that serve as influencers for Generation Z.

Gen Zers from English-Speaking (57%), Latin American (52%), and African-Islamic (51%) regions tended to be more influenced by their parents, when it comes to the decisions that they make. These findings are consistent with those from Mabille and Alom (2021) global study in which it was found that Gen Zers consider mothers as the most influential people in their lives, followed by friends, and then fathers.

Table 6.1. Influences on Decision-Making.

	Slightly Influences	Somewhat Influences	Greatly Influences
Parents/Guardians	14%	36%	47%
Siblings	24%	32%	21%
Other family members	33%	24%	10%

Table 6.2. Sources of Financial Information.

	Greatly Influences
Parents/guardians	84%
Online resources	39%
Friends/peers	31%
Social media	30%
Financial institutions	26%
Class	20%
Other family members	19%
Financial professional	11%

Note: The percentages do not total 100 as participants could select all that apply.

While they seek out advice from their family members on a variety of topics, parents, in particular, are the go-to for most Gen Zers (84%) when it comes to seeking financial information. As outlined in Table 6.2, parents, over all other people and places, are the number one resource for Gen Zers in acquiring financial information.

This is in alignment with the research from Mabille and Alom (2021) who note that 37% of Gen Zers talk to their fathers about money, and 30% get financial advice from their mothers.

As illuminated by the Global Gen Z Study, when looking at every region of the world, it is apparent that more Gen Zers seek financial advice from parents/guardians than any other source. While a slightly greater number of those are from English-speaking countries (90%), even the lowest percentage was just 74% in Africa.

Further, more Gen Zers seek out their mothers, specifically, than any other group of people to ask advice on religion, academics, feelings of meaninglessness, and future plans. A good number also get guidance on sexuality-related problems from their moms, only somewhat fewer than ask friends or physicians. Far fewer Gen Zers talk to either their fathers or siblings about any of these same issues (Mabille & Alom, 2021).

Gen Zers also play a role in influencing the decisions made by their families (Cruz et al., 2017; Puiu, 2016). Due to their tech-savvy nature, Gen Zers are adept at retrieving information (Tjiptono et al., 2020). They educate themselves about products and services, going deeper than acquiring just a superficial level of understanding (Puiu, 2016). With their technology-boosted knowledge and high expectations, Generation Z has the power to influence their parents, siblings, and friends in the consumption of goods and services such as with clothes, shoes, electronics, and food choices (Puiu, 2016). However, this does not extend to traveling decisions as they tend to be guided by the choices made by adults (Haddouche & Salomone, 2018). Overall, there appears to be a reciprocal relationship among Generation Z and their family, both influencing each other in making financial decisions.

Family Connection

According to Moral and Chimpén (2021), a healthy family is one in which members are interconnected while still having unique ideas, visions, and dreams. In particular, the COVID-19 pandemic illuminated the role and importance of a healthy family for Gen Zers. Twenty-eight percent of participants in the Global Gen Z Study reported moving in or remaining living with their family during the pandemic, which had the ability to foster closer connections among those in the household. In addition, many Gen Zers felt useful as they helped family members with technologies like digital media and new electronic gadgets (Mabille & Alom, 2021).

As for their future families, many in the Global Gen Z Study described a good life as one that would consist of happiness brought about by being part of a loving family. One Gen Zer wrote, "having a loyal partner who genuinely loves me, having a safe and healthy family..., [and] family to care about and love each other."

Conclusion

Family members are often the primary educators for children, being the first to socialize with them and protect them from harm. For Generation Z, family members have an immense influence on their decision-making and beliefs. Given this immense influence, parents and guardians, specifically, must continue to provide care and emotional warmth so as to foster life satisfaction and positive effect with their Generation Z children (Suldo & Fefer, 2013). But, it isn't just Gen Zers that want to receive this supportive parenting; they also want to give it. In the words of a Gen Zer from the Global Gen Z Study, a good life involves "having children and passing on my family name along with a long time generational family farm...knowing I left something behind when I go, but also being able to have enough memories to cherish when I am rocking in my chair gazing at [the lake] in my log cabin."

References

Alvarez, P. (2023). *Charted: The rapid decline of global birth rates.* https://www.visualcapitalist.com/cp/charted-rapid-decline-of-global-birth-rates/

Broadbent, E., Gougoulis, J., Lui, N., Pota, V., & Simons, J. (2017). Generation Z: Global citizenship survey. In *What the World's Young People Think and Feel.* https://www.varkeyfoundation.org/media/4487/global-young-people-report-single-pages-new.pdf

Council on Foreign Relations. (2022). *Marriage equality: Global comparisons.* https://www.cfr.org/backgrounder/marriage-equality-global-comparisons

Craig, L., & Mullan, K. (2011). How mothers and fathers share childcare: A cross-national time-use comparison. *American Sociological Review, 76*(6), 834–861. https://doi.org/10.1177/0003122411427673

Cruz, M., e Silva, S. C., & Machado, J. C. (2017). The influence of WOM and peer interaction in the decision-making process of Generation Z within the family. *International Journal of Marketing, Communication and New Media, 2,* 106–136.

Goodman, C. C. (2007). Family dynamics in three-generation grandfamilies. *Journal of Family Issues, 28*(3), 355–379.

Haddouche, H., & Salomone, C. (2018). Generation Z and the tourist experience: Tourist stories and use of social networks. *Journal of Tourism Futures, 4*(1), 69–79. https://doi.org/10.1108/JTF-12-2017-0059

Hall, K., & Mokomane, Z. (2018). The shape of children's families and households: A demographic overview. In K. Hall, L. Richter, Z. Mokomane, & L. Lake (Eds.), *South African child gauge 2018* (pp. 23–45). Children's Institute, University of Cape.

Huerta, M. C., Adema, W., Baxter, J., Han, W. J., Lausten, M., Lee, R., & Waldfogel, J. (2014). Fathers' leave and fathers' involvement: Evidence from four OECD countries. *European Journal of Social Security, 16*(4), 308–346. https://doi.org/10.1177/138826271401600403

Kuo, P. X., Volling, B. L., & Gonzalez, R. (2018). Gender role beliefs, work–family conflict, and father involvement after the birth of a second child. *Psychology of Men and Masculinity, 19*(2), 243.

Lin, C. (2021). More HDB households but average size shrank, with fewer multi-generational families living together. Channel News Asia. https://www.channelnewsasia.com/singapore/hdb-household-smaller-size-multi-generation-sample-survey-341896

Mabille, F., & Alom, M. (2021). *Towards a better understanding of youth's cultures & values (Working Paper) International Federation of Catholic Universities.* https://www.cirad-fiuc.org/wp-content/uploads/2021/05/WORKING-PAPER-version-web.pdf

Malone, K. (2007). The bubble-wrap generation: Children growing up in walled gardens. *Environmental Education Research, 13*(4), 513–527. https://doi.org/10.1080/13504620701581612

Masfety, V. K., Aarnink, C., Otten, R., Bitfoi, A., Mihova, Z., Lesinskiene, S., Carta, M. G., Goelitz, D., & Husky, M. (2019). Three-generation households and child mental health in European countries. *Social Psychiatry and Psychiatric Epidemiology, 54*(4), 427–436. https://doi.org/10.1007/s00127-018-1640-9

Miyazaki, R. (2021). A descriptive analysis of three-generation households and mothers' employment in Japan, 2002–2019. *International Journal of Sociology & Social Policy, 41*(13/14), 34–50.

Moral, M., & Chimpén, C. (2021). Developing and maintaining a healthy family today/Desarrollar y mantener una familiar sana hoy. *Revista de Psicoterapia, 32*, 197–210. https://doi.org/10.33898/rdp.v32i119.477

Oberle, E., Schonert-Reichl, K. A., & Zumbo, B. D. (2011). Life satisfaction in early adolescence: Personal, neighborhood, school, family, and peer influences. *Journal of Youth and Adolescence, 40*(7), 889–901. https://doi.org/10.1007/s10964-010-9599-1

OCSE. (2011). *Doing better for families.* OECD. https://www.oecd.org/social/soc/doingbetterforfamilies.htm

Oerther, S., & Oerther, D. B. (2021). Review of recent research about parenting Generation Z pre-teen children. *Western Journal of Nursing Research, 43*(11), 1073–1086. https://doi.org/10.1177/0193945920988782

Pilkauskas, N. V. (2012). Three-generation family households: Differences by family structure at birth. *Journal of Marriage and Family, 74*(5), 931–943. https://doi.org/10.1111/j.1741-3737.2012.01008.x

Puiu, S. (2016). Generation Z – A new type of consumers. *Young Economists Journal/Revista Tinerilor Economisti, 13*(27), 67–78.

Schneider, N. F., Kreyenfeld, M., Evertsson, M., Eriksson Kirsch, M., & Geerts, A. (2021). *Research handbook on the sociology of the family.* Edward Elgar Publishing.

Seemiller, C., & Grace, M. (2019). *Generation Z: A century in the making.* Routledge.

Skirbekk, V. (2022). *Decline and prosper! Changing global birth rates and the advantages of fewer children.* Springer Nature.

Suldo, S. M., & Fefer, S. A. (2013). Research, applications, and interventions for children and adolescents: A positive psychology perspective. In C. Proctor & P. A. Linley (Eds.), *Parent-child relationships and well-being* (pp. 131–147). Springer Science + Business Media. https://doi.org/10.1007/978-94-007-6398-2_8

Sumari, M., Subramaniam, S. D. R., & Md Khalid, N. (2020). Coping with parental divorce: A study of adolescents in a collectivist culture of Malaysia. *Journal of Divorce & Remarriage, 61*(3), 186–205. http://doi.org/10.1080/10502556.2019.1679595

Tamm, M. (2019). Fathers' parental leave-taking, childcare involvement and labor market participation. *Labour Economics, 59*, 184–197. https://doi.org/10.1016/j.labeco.2019.04.007

Tjiptono, F., Khan, G., Yeong, E. S., & Kunchamboo, V. (2020). Generation Z in Malaysia: The four 'E'generation. In E. Gentina & E. E. Parry (Eds.), *The new Generation Z in Asia: Dynamics, differences, digitalisation* (pp. 149–163). Emerald Publishing Limited.

Chapter 7

Navigating Interpersonal Dynamics

Corey Seemiller[a]*, Niva Dolev*[b] *and Meghan Grace*[c]

[a]Wright State University, USA
[b]Kinneret College on the Sea of Galilee, Israel
[c]Plaid, LLC, USA

Abstract

This chapter provides an overview of the factors influencing interpersonal dynamics in contemporary culture, including high levels of volatility, uncertainty, complexity, and ambiguity (VUCA), new technologies, growing competition for resources, highly diverse societies, and changing needs of professions and their likely effect on Generation Z's perspectives on interpersonal dynamics. Gen Zers prefer to do a task than lead it; like to work in groups; and are motivated by relational indicators. Overall, this is a generation that wants to come together to find solutions to epic challenges.

Keywords: Interpersonal relationships; communication; group dynamics; 21st century skills; emotional intelligence; social competence

In the last two decades, the world has been undergoing a revolution, typified by hyper-dynamic changes in all aspects of our lives (Mitra et al., 2016), and by higher levels of uncertainty, complexity, and ambiguity (VUCA) (Johansen & Euchner, 2013). Changes and consequent challenges include an exponential increase in knowledge and the ever-evolving invention of new technologies (Reis et al., 2019), coupled with limited resources, tighter regulations at the global level, and growing competition and interdependence (Fadel, 2008), as well as highly diverse societies (Greenstein, 2012) and the illuminating and rise of professions and changes in professional requirements and modes of employment for a variety of positions (McKinsey Global Institute, 2017). In addition, there is a call for a better understanding of the needs, expectations, and views of Generation Z (Seemiller & Clayton, 2019), including their communication styles and the nature of relationships.

Gen Z Around the World, 61–68
Published under exclusive licence by Emerald Publishing Limited
doi:10.1108/978-1-83797-092-620241007

To be able to cope with these changes and prepare those who are still to come, a wide set of skills is required. Alongside technical, professional, and technological skills, young people today will need to develop personal, emotional, and social skills. Possessing these skills will enable them to adapt to changes in the workplace, manage challenging tasks, be able to discern the appropriateness and legitimacy of information from a vast amount of available content, and apply that knowledge across their varied life roles (Ananiadou & Claro, 2009) while building relationships, communicating and collaborating with others locally and globally, and providing personalized solutions and services. Human connection and interpersonal relations are more important than ever in a changing world.

Interpersonal Skills

Alongside intrapersonal competencies such as resilience, growth mindset, problem-solving, critical thinking, curiosity and passion, creativity, and innovation are interpersonal skills such as empathy, building and maintaining positive relationships, collaboration and communication, teamwork, and care about the well-being of others and the planet (Deming, 2017; OECD, 2018; Turiman et al., 2012). These interpersonal skills are critical for meeting the needs of the emerging developments of the century (Ananiadou & Claro, 2009).

Further, such skills are often included in the concept of social–emotional competence (SEC), defined as the essential social and emotional knowledge, skills, attitudes, mindset, and action that individuals need to succeed in life (Osher et al., 2016). Goleman (2020) noted that with all the advancements in society, SECs are no longer being transferred naturally to younger generations as in the past and need to be cultivated intentionally.

SEC originated from the concept of emotional intelligence (EI) and is defined as "the subset of social intelligence that involves the ability to monitor one's own and others' feelings and emotions, to discriminate among them and to use this information to guide one's thinking and actions" (Salovey et al., 2004, p. 5). Others describe EI as the skills which impact upon behaviors and outcomes, including interpersonal relations. For example, Bar-On (2006) included interpersonal skills (empathy, interpersonal relations, and social responsibility) as one of the five main areas of EI. For example, individuals' general levels of positivity, assertiveness, and impulse-control may impact their interpersonal relationships (Stein & Book, 2011). In particular, it has been noted that emotions have a big impact on interpersonal relationships (Machová et al., 2020). In fact, the study of EI emerged as a type of social intelligence (Thorndike, 1920; Wechsler, 1939) claiming that people differ from each other in the ways they deal with their emotions and their manifestations in social interactions.

One of the main factors influencing emotional and social intelligence is the environment, including culture. Thus, generational differences in terms of EI can be expected because environments and cultures evolve for each generational cohort. A recent study indicated that Gen Zers consider EI more important in life than cognitive intelligence, valuing EI more than any other generation; they, however, had the lowest actual EI levels of all generations (Machová et al., 2020). In contrast, another study found that EI and social intelligence for Turkish Gen Zers, in particular, was above the average across other age groups (Ordun et al., 2021). These conflicting findings could be attributed to the complexity of EI in that one may have a higher level of self-awareness yet a lower level of interpersonal competence. For Generation Z, this may be a plausible explanation in that they may have differentiated skillsets regarding the various components of EI.

According to Bar-On (2006), three EI skills fall under interpersonal skills. These include empathy, interpersonal relationships, and social responsibility. While these specific skills were not measured specifically in the Global Gen Z Study, participants were able to evaluate the extent that a list of 35 characteristics described them. In looking specifically at the seven characteristics that correspond with Bar-On's (2006) interpersonal skills, Table 7.1 includes the percentage of those who indicated that the characteristic greatly describes them.

It appears that Gen Zers from the Global Gen Z Study have a stronger identification with the characteristics affiliated with the Empathy category over the Interpersonal Relationships category. Empathy appears to reflect an internal process of interpersonal skills, whereas Interpersonal Relationships reflect an external process of interacting with others. Social responsibility is mixed in that Inclusive is lower than other characteristics, yet Loyal was the highest.

In looking by World Values Region, of all interpersonal characteristics, Loyal had the highest percentages for all nine regions. And, for most regions, Loyal had the highest percentage of all 35 characteristics listed, not just those associated with interpersonal skills. With Loyal being a characteristic that Gen Zers see themselves possessing, it makes sense that one of the top five sources of motivation includes Not Wanting To Let Others Down.

What Matters in Their Relationships

When older generations came of age, many formed friendships and even romantic relationships based on who lived near each other or who was on a sports team or in a club together, in essence, proximity and shared hobbies. With the proliferation of technology today, it's no surprise that neither of these factors holds a great deal of weight for Generation Z. They are able to connect with people from all over the world, with diverse interests. It's not surprising then that findings from the Global Gen Z Study found proximity and shared culture as being less

Table 7.1. Bar-On EI Framework and Gen Z Characteristics.

Bar-On EI Framework	Gen Z Characteristics
Empathy	Compassionate (62%)
	Thoughtful (63%)
Interpersonal relationships	Collaborative (48%)
	Communicative (40%)
	Cooperative (53%)
Social responsibility	Inclusive (49%)
	Loyal (77%)

important for fostering interpersonal relationships than shared values, which is the most important factor among Gen Zers in every world region. The importance of values may be grounded in connection and trust that goes deeper than playing together in the neighborhood or warming up on the basketball team. It's not surprising then that the biggest influencers in their lives are those people that they do share a close connection with, and arguably a similar set of values. The number one influencer, globally, for Generation Z is their parents with 47% indicating they are greatly influenced by them. The second highest was siblings at 21%, followed by friends/peers at 20% and teachers/professors at 14%. The lowest four are groups that tend to fall outside of one's social circle: social media influencers (2%), politicians (2%), celebrities (3%), and professional athletes (4%).

Interpersonal Skills

While Gen Zers prefer face-to-face communication (Seemiller & Grace, 2016), many are worried that they may lack important skills that allow them to interact with and communicate effectively with others (Seemiller & Grace, 2019). Their lack of skills stems from a growing reliance on technology and social media (Seemiller & Grace, 2019), having less time practicing social skills than previous generations (Twenge et al., 2019), which was exacerbated by the pandemic, as well as a reluctance in acknowledging their mistakes in times of conflict, often aiming to avoid saying anything that could make a conflict escalate (Pečiuliauskienė, 2018).

Group Work

Social intelligence is the ability to work effectively with others (Seal et al., 2006) and is critical for work success (World Economic Forum, 2021; National Association of Colleges and Employers, 2020). Overall, those in Generation Z like working with others. The 75% in the Global Gen Z Study who indicated enjoying or somewhat enjoying group work reported it was because they like sharing the workload with others, meeting and getting to work with people, and getting new ideas and perspectives. One Gen Zer from the study said, "I like that it's so many different perspectives coming together to work on one idea."

On the other hand, 25% indicated not enjoying group work very much or at all. Reasons included having to deal with others not following through, having an uneven workload, trusting and relying on others, and generally having to interact with people. One participant summed up the sentiment by saying, "It just tends to complicate the process, and I end up putting in more than I get out." While there is a difference between these percentages regionally, ranging from 68 to 86%, the vast majority of Gen Zers in every region actually enjoy group work.

Interestingly, findings from the Global Gen Z Study highlight a relationship between feelings about group work and optimistic attitudes. At the global level, 60% of those who noted enjoying group work also indicated believing people are inherently good versus only 33% who marked that they didn't like group work. Further, only 38% who like group work believe people will let them down compared to 63% of those who don't enjoy working in groups. Overall Gen Zers like group work. But, it is those with higher optimism levels that tend to look more favorably on it.

Group Roles

In regard to working with others, Gen Zers, on both a global level and dis-aggregated to regional levels, prefer certain group roles. The four roles measured in the Global Gen Z Study were replicated from earlier research (Seemiller & Grace, 2016) and include:

- Leading – taking charge/initiative, setting the tone for the group, influencing others.
- Doing – executing tasks, getting things done, following direction, meeting deadlines, creating routine.
- Relating – connecting with others, including others, developing others, demonstrating empathy and harmony.
- Thinking – analyzing, planning, researching, collecting information, asking "why?", synthesizing information.

These four roles were labeled uniquely but align with the four quadrants of the Gallup Strengths, which include the Executing domain (Doing), Influencing domain (Leading), Relationship Building domain (Relating), and Strategic Thinking domain (Thinking) (Gallup, n.d.).

Findings from the Global Gen Z Study show that 76% often or always engage in Doing, 76% in Thinking, 66% in Relating, and 46% in Leading. In looking at these roles by World Values Regions (World Values Survey Association, 2022), the trends are consistent with the global findings. Doing ranked as the most prominent role with Confucian, African-Islamic, English-speaking, Protestant European, and African countries, whereas Thinking ranked the highest for Orthodox Europe and Catholic Europe. Only the West and South Asia region ranked Relating first. Given the nearly equal representation globally between Doing and Thinking, it makes sense to see this regional distribution. While Relating was found to be unique to West and South Asia, Leading was not a prominent style among Gen Zers in any world region.

Relational Motivators

Twenty-two measurements from the Motivation Indicator were used to assess motivators of Generation Z (Seemiller, 2009). Of the 22 measurements, eight represented extrinsic rationale, seven represented intrinsic, and seven represented relational. Of the 10 highest rated motivators from the Global Gen Z study listed in Table 7.2, only two are in the relational category, Not Wanting To Let Others Down and Making a Difference For Someone Else. Further, five were intrinsic

Table 7.2. Highest Rated Motivators.

Motivator	Category
Seeing the fruits of your labor/accomplishment	Intrinsic
Having an opportunity for advancement	Extrinsic
Advocating for something you believe in	Intrinsic
Learning something or being better at something	Intrinsic
Not wanting to let others down	Relational
Wanting to do well because you committed	Intrinsic
Making a difference for someone else	Relational
Receiving tangible rewards	Extrinsic
Gaining experience to build your resume	Extrinsic
Caring about the project or task	Intrinsic

and three were extrinsic, indicating that relationships may be one of the lower motivators overall.

In all regions but Africa, Not Wanting To Let Others Down shows up in the top 10, and in six of the nine regions, Making a Difference For Someone Else is ranked in the top 10. Individual recognition emerged in Confucian countries, Catholic Europe, and Protestant Europe. And, pleasing others was prevalent in Protestant Europe, while feeling the need to be loyal to the values of your community was present in Confucian countries. While there is some variance, what is most noticeable is that there is a lot more similarity in terms of relational motivators. This is a generation that is motivated to do something if they know that what they are doing will help someone else. What is also telling is that of the top 10 motivators only one to three of them, depending on the region, are reflective of relational motivators. This lack of relational motivators on a global and regional level highlights that this generation primarily likes to be motivated intrinsically rather than relationally.

Conclusion

Overall, there are far more similarities globally with Generation Z regarding how they see and approach interpersonal and group dynamics. Collectively, they have a great sense of loyalty, thoughtfulness, and compassion, highlighting their commitment to interpersonal connection. Finding ways to help them develop and foster relationships with others will be critical to their success and happiness.

They also seek relationships with people who have shared values and believe those in their inner circles are the ones most influential to them. Knowing this may help those who teach, supervise, coach, or develop members of this generation as those individuals serve as important influencers themselves and can understand and leverage the influence that others in Generation Z's inner circle play in their decision-making.

Overall, a vast majority of those in Generation Z like working in groups. It is clear, though, that by engaging in more Doing and Thinking roles than Relating and even more so, Leading, they see themselves more as everyday workers versus the initiators or leaders. Thus, it is important for those working with Generation Z to help them develop social–emotional skills and confidence to effectively lead, work in groups, and prepare them for the unknown future (Ananiadou & Claro, 2009; Dolev & Itzkovich, 2020).

While those in Generation Z seem to prefer intrinsic motivators, when they are motivated by relationships, it is often because they don't want to let others down and ultimately want to make a difference in others' lives. Understanding these relational motivations can help those working with Generation Z structure group work, service projects, and work initiatives that highlight impact on others.

References

Ananiadou, K., & Claro, M. (2009). *21st century skills and competences for new millennium learners in OECD countries*. OECD, EDU Working paper no. 41. https://doi.org/10.1787/19939019

Bar-On, R. (2006). The Bar-On model of emotional-social intelligence (ESI). *Psicothema, 18*(1), 13–25.

Deming, D. J. (2017). The growing importance of social skills in the labor market. *The Quarterly Journal of Economics, 132*(4), 1593–1640. https://doi.org/10.1093/qje/qjx022

Dolev, N., & Itzkovich, Y. (2020). In the AI era soft skills are the new hard skills. In W. Amann & W. Stachowicz-Stanusch (Eds.), *Artificial intelligence and its impact on business* (pp. 55–77). Information Age Publishing.

Fadel, C. (2008). 21st century skills: How can you prepare students for the new global economy. In *Partnership for 21stCentury skills*. OECD/CERI Paris. https://ams-forschungsnetzwerk.at/downloadpub/40756908.pdf

Gallup. (n.d.). *What are the four domains of CliftonStrengths?* https://www.gallup.com/cliftonstrengths/en/253736/cliftonstrengths-domains.aspx

Goleman, D. (2020). *Emotional intelligence* (25th Anniversary edition). Bloomsbury.

Greenstein, L. M. (2012). *Assessing 21st century skills: A guide to evaluating mastery and authentic learning*. Corwin Press.

Johansen, B., & Euchner, J. (2013). Navigating the VUCA world. *Research-Technology Management, 56*(1), 10–15. https://doi.org/10.5437/08956308X5601003

Machová, R., Zsigmond, T., Lazányl, K. & Krepszová, V. (2020). Generations and emotional intelligence a pilot study. *Acta Polytechnica Hungarica, 17*(5), 229–247.

McKinsey Global Institute. (2017). *Jobs lost, jobs gained: Workplace transitions in the time of automation*. McKinsey and Company. https://www.mckinsey.com/~/media/mckinsey/industries/public%20and%20social%20sector/our%20insights/what%20the%20future%20of%20work%20will%20mean%20for%20jobs%20skills%20and%20wages/mgi%20jobs%20lost-jobs%20gained_report_december%202017.pdf

Mitra, S., Kulkarni, S., & Stanfield, J. (2016). Learning at the edge of chaos: Self-organizing systems in education. In H. E. Lees & N. Noddings (Eds.), *The*

Palgrave international handbook of alternative education (pp. 227–239). Palgrave Macmillan.

National Association of Colleges and Employers. (2020). Job outlook 2021. https://www.naceweb.org/store/2020/job-outlook-2021/

OECD. (2018). *Education 2030: The future of education and skills – The future we want.* https://www.oecd.org/education/2030/E2030%20Position%20Paper%20(05.04.2018).pdf

Ordun, G., Ozeren, C. G., & Mercimek, K. (2021). Social, cultural, emotional intelligence and entrepreneurial intention: A research on Generation Z. *Journal of Organizational Behavior Review, 3*(2), 222–240.

Osher, D., Kidron, Y., Brackett, M., Dymnicki, A., Jones, S., & Weissberg, R. P. (2016). Advancing the science and practice of social and emotional learning: Looking back and moving forward. *Review of Research in Education, 40*(1), 644–681. https://doi.org/10.3102/0091732X16673595

Pečiuliauskienė, P. (2018). The structure of interpersonal communication skills of the new generation senior school students: The case of Generations X and Z. *Pedagogika, 130*(2), 116–130. https://doi.org/10.15823/p.2018.26

Reis, M., Matos, M. G., & Ramiro, L. (2019). Worries, mental and emotional health difficulties of Portuguese university students. *Advances in Social Sciences Research Journal, 6*(7), 558–569. http://doi.org/10.14738/assrj.67.6818

Salovey, P., Brackett, M. A., & Meyer, J. D. (2004). *Emotional intelligence.* Dude Publishing.

Seal, C. R., Boyatzis, R. E., & Bailey, J. R. (2006). Fostering emotional and social intelligence in organizations. *Organization Management Journal, 3*(3), 190–209. https://doi.org/10.1057/omj.2006.19

Seemiller, C. (2009). *Motivation indicator.* Unpublished manuscript. The University of Arizona.

Seemiller, C., & Clayton, J. (2019). Developing the strengths of Generation Z college students. *Journal of College and Character, 20*(3), 268–275. https://doi.org/10.1080/2194587X.2019.1631187

Seemiller, C., & Grace, M. (2016). *Generation Z goes to college.* Jossey-Bass.

Seemiller, C., & Grace, M. (2019). *Generation Z: A century in the making.* Routledge.

Stein, S. J., & Book, H. E. (2011). *The EQ edge: Emotional intelligence and your success.* John Wiley & Sons.

Thorndike, E. L. (1920). Intelligence and its uses. *Harper's Magazine, 140,* 227–235.

Turiman, P., Omar, J., Daud, A. M., & Osman, K. (2012). Fostering the 21st century skills through scientific literacy and science process skills. *Procedia-Social and Behavioral Sciences, 59,* 110–116. http://doi.org/10.1016/j.sbspro.2012.09.253

Twenge, J. M., Spitzberg, B. H., & Campbell, W. K. (2019). Less in-person social interaction with peers among U.S. adolescents in the 21st century and links to loneliness. *Journal of Social and Personal Relationships, 36*(6), 1892–1913. https://doi.org/10.1177/0265407519836170

Wechsler, D. (1939). *The measurement of adult intelligence.* Williams & Witkins.

World Economic Forum. (2021). What is 'The Great Resignation'? An expert explains. https://www.weforum.org/agenda/2021/11/what-is-the-great-resignation-and-what-can-we-learn-from-it/

World Values Survey Association. (2022). World values survey. https://www.worldvaluessurvey.org/WVSContents.jsp

Chapter 8

Learning Preferences

Corey Seemiller[a] and Meghan Grace[b]

[a]Wright State University, USA
[b]Plaid, LLC, USA

Abstract

This chapter explores Generation Z's perceptions of learning. Learning can be viewed from three distinct lenses: effectiveness, enjoyment, and engagement of various modalities. Modalities include demonstrated (watch in person), video-based (watch online), intrapersonal (independent), interpersonal (in collaboration with others), social (among others but not working together), and experiential (doing). Effectiveness involves the extent that a certain modality is effective for learning. Enjoyment is reflective of preference and satisfaction with different modalities. Finally, engagement is the actual utilization of specific modalities.

Keywords: Learning; modalities; pedagogy; learning preferences; instructional strategies; perceptions of learning

Curious and open-minded – two distinct characteristics that Gen Zers from across the globe say describe themselves. And, they aren't just open to new ideas; they are motivated by enhancing their knowledge and skills, emanating their passion and readiness to learn.

Learning can be viewed from three distinct lenses: effectiveness, enjoyment, and engagement. Effectiveness involves the extent that a certain modality is effective for learning. Enjoyment is reflective of preference and satisfaction with different modalities. Finally, engagement is the actual utilization of specific modalities.

Learning Methods

There are a variety of learning modalities that can be applied to achieve effectiveness, enjoyment, and engagement. Those used in the Global Gen Z Study include

Gen Z Around the World, 69–78
Copyright © 2024 Corey Seemiller and Meghan Grace
Published under exclusive licence by Emerald Publishing Limited
doi:10.1108/978-1-83797-092-620241008

demonstrated, video-based, intrapersonal, interpersonal, social, and experiential learning. These categories were derived from qualitative findings from the Generation Z Goes to College study in 2014 (Seemiller & Grace, 2016).

Demonstrated Learning

Demonstrated learning involves watching someone perform a task that needs to be replicated. This might take the form of a lab demonstration in the sciences, doing a mock case study with the whole class before assigning a different case study for an assignment, or even showing, step-by-step, how to complete a statistical analysis. Demonstrations have been found to garner interest and elicit enjoyment from students as many often consider them highlights of their learning experiences (Kestin et al., 2020). However, demonstrations, if not done correctly or if they fail to produce the intended results, can be a confusing and ineffective method of learning (Kestin et al., 2020).

Video-Based Learning

Video-based learning involves learning content by watching videos. While this type of learning could also include demonstrated learning in which someone records themselves performing a task, video-based learning can also include recorded lectures, interactive modules, and games. In terms of effectiveness, combined with reading, watching videos has been found to increase exam scores for students (Bassett et al., 2020). Watching recorded videos has been found to motivate students to learn (Prabhath et al., 2022). Further, online demonstrations versus live ones have been found to be more effective for learning, based on student test scores, as well as more enjoyable for students (Kestin et al., 2020). Regarding enjoyment, students appear to be more satisfied and have more positive attitudes regarding video books over printed textbooks (Granitz et al., 2021). Further, Gen Z students, in particular, enjoy "podcasts, websites, simulations, interactive tutorials on YouTube, and Internet-based educational games" (Hernandez-de-Menendez et al., 2020, p. 850). In a study of Generation Z nursing students, video-based learning was their third most preferred and third most effective learning modality out of 13 options, with 61% and 67%, respectively, indicating so (Hampton et al., 2020).

Intrapersonal Learning

Intrapersonal learning involves learning on one's own, often in a self-paced, independent manner. In determining effectiveness, a study by Bassett et al. (2020) found that when combined with watching videos, reading has been found to positively impact student test scores (Bassett et al., 2020). Intrapersonal learning, such as viewing slides before a lecture, can also serve as a motivating factor for learning (Prabhath et al., 2022). In a study of US Generation Z college students by Seemiller and Grace (2016), nearly 52% reported that intrapersonal learning is greatly effective, higher than any other method in the study, including interpersonal learning (Seemiller & Grace, 2016). For enjoyment, Gen Zers also demonstrate higher levels of satisfaction when they can complete work on their own timeline (DiMattio, 2020). In terms of engagement, Shorey et al. (2021) found that Gen Z health-care students mostly participate in independent learning.

Interpersonal Learning

Interpersonal learning occurs when individuals engage in collaboration and team-based learning. This modality has been found to be more effective than other methods in students' acquisition of higher grades (Dass et al., 2021). In addition to effectiveness, Gen Zers prefer collaborative learning as one of the main modalities to assist in their learning (Naim, 2021). But findings aren't consistent between effectiveness and enjoyment. In a study of nursing students, 38% preferred to learn through collaborative projects, whereas only 27% believed collaboration was an effective modality (Hampton et al., 2020).

Social Learning

Social learning involves learning around, but not with or from others. It usually looks like a quiet group of individuals all working independently but near each other. It involves a mix of independent learning and group learning where students can toggle back and forth between the two modalities. Those in Generation Z believe that other learners must be focused, serious, and not distracting (Seemiller & Grace, 2016). Further, more than 26% of participants, when asked to describe their ideal learning environment in their own words, indicated the effectiveness of social learning (Seemiller & Grace, 2016). One participant discussed the importance of being surrounded by "multiple intellectuals cooperating together to solve problems and discuss issues" (Seemiller & Grace, 2014, row 131).

Experiential Learning

Experiential learning occurs when students learn by practicing or engaging in a skill. This can occur through applied learning, for instance, taking something learned in class and applying it to an internship. It can also occur through hands-on learning in a classroom where students can practice implementing concepts they learned, through case studies, roleplaying, makerspaces, etc. In terms of enjoyment, Gen Zers agree that applied learning, in particular, can help them determine how their interests and skills line up with their future careers (Gallup/Bates, 2019).

However, not all Gen Zers like experiential learning. In a study by Manzoni et al., younger learners prefer "abstract conceptualization and reflective observation," whereas older generations prefer "active experimentation and concrete experience," which debunks generational stereotypes of Gen Zers preferring experiential learning over other learning methods (2021, p. 55). As for engagement, though, Shorey et al. (2021) found that health-care students, in particular, are drawn to participating in active learning.

Effectiveness, Enjoyment, and Engagement

In looking specifically at the entire global cohort data from the Global Gen Z Study, Gen Zers were able to select, for each of the six modalities, whether they consider the modality effective for learning (effectiveness), enjoy the modality (enjoyment), and/or often engage in that modality (engagement). They were able to select all that apply for each modality. The percentage listed in Table 8.1 includes those who selected responses for effectiveness, enjoyment, and engagement.

Learning Interdependently Versus Independently

The modalities noted with the highest rates of effectiveness appear to be those that involve learning by doing (experiential) or watching others do (demonstrated). This reflects their desire for real-life application and step-by-step instructions inherent in both of these modalities. Enjoyment, on the other hand, is marked by high levels of learning with (interpersonal) or around (social) others. Finally, the modalities Gen Zers indicated engaging in most included high levels of self-direction and independent work (video-based and intrapersonal). However, COVID-19 may have contributed to an overinflation of rates of engagement in the video-based and intrapersonal learning modalities since many students were or had recently engaged in independent learning through remote and virtual options during the time of the survey completion (Ferri et al., 2020; Prabhath et al., 2022).

Table 8.1. Effectiveness, Enjoyment, and Engagement.

Modality	Effectiveness	Enjoyment	Engagement
Experiential	38%	34%	28%
Demonstrated	>37%	36%	27%
Interpersonal	<37%	39%	24%
Social	34%	42%	24%
Video-based	34%	37%	30%
Intrapersonal	31%	31%	37%

Inconsistencies Between Effectiveness and Engagement

When comparing rates within each learning modality, it appears that intrapersonal learning has consistent rates of effectiveness and enjoyment. A higher
percentage of Gen Zers find social, interpersonal, and video-based learning
enjoyable but not as many see them as effective learning modalities. On the other
hand, experiential and demonstrated learning have higher rates of effectiveness
than they do enjoyment. In all cases, except intrapersonal learning, engagement
levels were found to be lower than effectiveness and enjoyment. What these
findings point to is either making more effective modalities more enjoyable as well
as more enjoyable modalities more effective.

Learning Modalities Across Regions

Given the diversity between each of the associated regional cultures according to
the World Values Survey (World Values Survey Association, 2022), one might

Table 8.2. Top Three Modalities for Each Region.

	Effectiveness	Enjoyment	Engagement
Africa[a]	Demonstrated (35%)	Video-based (49%)	Intrapersonal (40%)
	Experiential (35%)	Social (44%)	Social (33%)
	Interpersonal (35%)	Demonstrated (39%)	Interpersonal (30%)
African-Islamic	Experiential (40%)	Social (41%)	Intrapersonal (31%)
	Demonstrated (38%)	Interpersonal (40%)	Video-based (30%)
	Interpersonal (34%)	Video-based (39%)	Social (27%)
Catholic Europe	Demonstrated (39%)	Social (42%)	Intrapersonal (41%)
	Interpersonal (39%)	Interpersonal (38%)	Video-based (28%)
	Experiential (39%)	Demonstrated (35%)	Experiential (28%)
Confucian	Experiential (41%)	Social (42%)	Intrapersonal (46%)
	Interpersonal (34%)	Experiential (42%)	Video-based (43%)
	Social (31%)	Interpersonal (39%)	Demonstrated (32%)

Table 8.2. *(Continued)*

	Effectiveness	Enjoyment	Engagement
English-Speaking	Experiential (37%) Demonstrated (35%) Interpersonal (34%)	Social (41%) Interpersonal (39%) Video-based (37%)	Intrapersonal (35%) Video-based (31%) Experiential (29%)
Latin America	Demonstrated (35%) Interpersonal (34%) Experiential (34%)	Social (45%) Interpersonal (42%) Video-based (42%)	Experiential (34%) Intrapersonal (30%) Demonstrated (27%)
Orthodox Europe	Interpersonal (40%) Demonstrated (38%) Experiential (37%)	Social (43%) Interpersonal (39%) Video-based (37%)	Intrapersonal (38%) Experiential (32%) Demonstrated (28%)
Protestant Europe	Interpersonal (46%) Experiential (43%) Demonstrated (41%)	Social (45%) Interpersonal (40%) Demonstrated (36%)	Intrapersonal (44%) Video-based (32%) Demonstrated (22%)
West and South Asia	Experiential (39%) Video-based (37%) Demonstrated (35%)	Social (43%) Interpersonal (40%) Demonstrated (33%)	Video-based (41%) Intrapersonal (37%) Experiential (33%)

[a]Not included in the World Values Survey.

expect differences regarding the highest ranked learning modalities for effectiveness, enjoyment, and engagement. Table 8.2 includes the top three modalities, with percentages, for effectiveness, enjoyment, and engagement.

Consistency Across Regions

Even when disaggregating by region, there is ample consistency as to what Gen Zers deem the most effective learning modalities. For instance, all regions rank experiential learning in their top three; eight of nine rank demonstrated and interpersonal learning; one of nine rank social learning; and none rank intrapersonal learning. These findings point to a global Gen Z cohorts that finds learning by doing or watching as well as learning with others as effective but not learning alone or learning independently in the company of others. While these findings may reflect a dissatisfaction of the shift to e-learning during the pandemic and a craving for hands-on learning and interpersonal connection, two modalities that were likely scaled back during the pandemic, it is important to note that postpandemic, Gen Zers want connection, interaction, and application.

In terms of enjoyment, there is a great deal of consistency as well. All regions rank social learning in their top three; eight of nine rank interpersonal; one of nine rank experiential learning; and none rank intrapersonal learning. The nuance in regard to enjoyment is with video-based learning. All include it in their top three, with the exception of both Asian regions and all of Europe except Eastern Europe.

Despite geopolitical, historical, and cultural nuances, how Gen Zers view learning is similar given other global similarities. Perhaps this is due to the ever-expanding "era of technology and communication," which is resulting in greater worldwide accessibility to the internet (Wargadinata et al., 2020, p. 142) or globalization in which multinational companies, nearly geographically limitless tech platforms, and constant travel and communication make it easier than ever to share some element of modern culture that cuts across a multitude of nations. Further, the pandemic accelerated globalization as health, trade, economies, and the labor force were all interconnected and necessitated a coordinated response (Sforza & Steininger, 2020). And, the general response to learning globally has included more online synchronous and asynchronous learning and an increased reliance on digital resources in place of face-to-face interaction (Ferri et al., 2020).

With engagement, though, there is less overall consistency other than all regions ranking intrapersonal learning in their top three, and none ranking interpersonal learning. However, experiential learning, for instance, emerged in the top three for five regions. There does not appear to be an obvious pattern for the regions this finding emerged versus those that it didn't. Similarly, unpatterned responses occurred with demonstrated and video-based learning as well. Further research may be necessary to explain the rationale behind these findings.

Inconsistencies Across Effectiveness, Enjoyment, and Engagement

It appears that at the regional level, interpersonal learning is viewed as effective and enjoyable but has lower engagement levels, and intrapersonal learning as not as effective or enjoyable but has higher engagement levels. Clearly, learners don't engage in as much interpersonal learning as they would like and perhaps engage in more intrapersonal learning than they would prefer. Again, this is likely a

Table 8.3. Number of Regions With Top Three Learning Modalities.

Modality	Effectiveness	Enjoyment	Engagement
Demonstrated	89% (8/9)	44% (4/9)	44% (4/9)
Experiential	100% (9/9)	11% (1/9)	56% (5/9)
Social	11% (1/9)	100% (9/9)	22% (2/9)
Interpersonal	89% (8/9)	89% (8/9)	11% (1/9)
Intrapersonal	0% (0/9)	0% (0/9)	100% (9/9)
Video-based	11% (1/9)	56% (5/9)	67% (6/9)

residual reaction from the stark shift to e-learning during the pandemic, where interpersonal modalities were nearly abandoned out of safety precautions.

More Gen Zers also see demonstrated and experiential learning as more effective than enjoyable, whereas the opposite is true for social and video-based learning. This may be explained in that learning by doing and watching can offer clarification for how to do a task, which supports Shorey et al.'s (2021) findings, in that students see experiential learning as effective. On the other hand, social learning and video-based learning may be predisposed to be fun, given its propensity to be interpersonally connecting and/or entertaining. Table 8.3 includes the number of regions, out of nine, that included each learning modality in its top three.

Conclusion

There are three main takeaways. First, it appears that there is far more similarity in terms of Gen Zers' views on learning regardless of their geographic region or cultural background. Given that, there could be more universal educator preparation programs and learning resources designed that would meet the needs of Generation Z across cultures and nations.

Second, interpersonal learning was seen as both effective and enjoyable while intrapersonal learning was less so for both. Given that in previous studies, intrapersonal learning ranked higher than interpersonal learning (Seemiller & Grace, 2014), perhaps, in the postpandemic world, young people are tiring of self-directed, self-paced, and independent learning and are craving group interaction.

Third, aside from interpersonal and intrapersonal learning, other modalities, such as experiential and social learning, lacked consistency between perceptions of being effective and enjoyable. Educators may need to explore ways to make those learning modalities of preference more effective and modalities of effectiveness more enjoyable.

As modalities of learning are dynamic and ever-changing, it is important to stay on the pulse of what learners want. Gen Zers are no exception. Given they are clear about what they find effective, enjoy, and engage in, their insight can offer guidance to educators to best design and offer learning experiences that meet their needs.

References

Bassett, K., Olbricht, G. R., & Shannon, K. B. (2020). Student preclass preparation by both reading the textbook and watching videos online improves exam performance in a partially flipped course. *CBE-Life Sciences Education, 19*(3), 1–9. https://doi.org/10.1187/cbe.19-05-0094

Dass, S., Ramananda, H. S., Jagadeesha, B., Rajesh Kumar, P. C., & Cherian, R. K. (2021). Effectiveness of collaborative on learning among Gen Z engineering students. *Journal of Engineering Education Transformations, 34*(3), 70–78. ISSN 2349-2473, eISSN 2394-1707.

DiMattio, M. J. K. (2020). Educating Generation Z: Psychosocial dimensions of the clinical learning environment that predict student satisfaction. *Nurse Education in Practice, 49*. Article 102902. https://doi.org/10.1016/j.nepr.2020.102901

Ferri, F., Grifoni, P., & Guzzo, T. (2020). Online learning and emergency remote teaching: Opportunities and challenges in emergency situations. *Societies, 10*(86). https://doi.org/10.3390/soc10040086

Gallup/Bates. (2019). *Forging pathways to purposeful work.* https://www.gallup.com/education/248222/gallup-bates-purposeful-work-2019.aspx

Granitz, N., Kohli, C., & Lancellotti, M. P. (2021). Textbooks for the YouTube generation? A case study on the shift from text to video. *The Journal of Education for Business, 96*(5), 299–307. https://doi.org/10.1080/08832323.2020.1828791

Hampton, D., Welsh, D., & Wiggins, A. T. (2020). Learning preferences and engagement level of Generation Z nursing students. *Nurse Educator, 45*(3), 160–164. https://doi.org/10.1097/NNE.0000000000000710

Hernandez-de-Menendez, M., Escobar Díaz, C. A., & Morales-Menendez, R. (2020). Educational experiences with Generation Z. *International Journal on Interactive Design and Manufacturing (IJIDeM), 14*(3), 847–859.

Kestin, G., Miller, K., McCarty, L. S., Callaghan, K., & Deslauriers, L. (2020). Comparing the effectiveness of online versus live lecture demonstrations. *Physical Review Physics Education Research, 16*(1), 013101. https://doi.org/10.1103/PhysRevPhysEducRes.16.013101

Manzoni, B., Caporarello, L., Cirulli, F., & Magni, F. (2021). The preferred learning styles of Generation Z: Do they differ from the ones of previous generations? In C. Metallo, M. Ferrara, A. Lazazzara, & S. Za (Eds.), *Digital transformation and human behavior, Lecture Notes in Information Systems and Organisation* (Vol. 37, pp. 55–67). https://doi.org/10.1007/978-3-030-47539-0_5

Naim, M. F. (2021). Exploring learning preferences of Gen Z employees: A conceptual analysis. In *Applications of work integrated learning among Gen Z and Y students* (pp. 1–14). IGI Global. https://doi.org/10.4018/978-1-7998-6440-0.ch001

Prabhath, S., DSouza, A., Pandey, A. K., Pandey, A. K., & Prasanna, L. C. (2022). Changing paradigms in anatomy teaching-learning during a pandemic: Modification of curricular delivery based on student perspectives. *Journal of Taibah University Medical Sciences, 17*(3), 488–497. https://doi.org/10.1016/j.jtumed.2021.10.014

Seemiller, C., & Grace, M. (2014). *Generation Z goes to college.* Unpublished data set.

Seemiller, C., & Grace, M. (2016). *Generation Z goes to college*. Jossey-Bass.

Sforza, A., & Steininger, M. (2020). *Globalization in the time of COVID-19*. Munich Society for the Promotion of Economic Research – CESifo GmbH. ISSN 2364-1428.

Shorey, S., Chan, V., Rajendran, P., & Ang, E. (2021). Learning styles, preferences and needs of Generation Z healthcare students: Scoping review. *Nurse Education in Practice, 57*, 103247.

Wargadinata, I., Maimunah, I., Dewi, E., & Rofiq, Z. (2020). Student's responses on learning in the early COVID-19 pandemic. *Tadris: Journal of Education and Teacher Training, 5*(1), 141–153. https://doi.org/10.24042/tadris.v5i1.6153

World Values Survey Association. (2022). *World values survey*. https://www.worldvaluessurvey.org/WVSContents.jsp

Chapter 9

Health, Nutrition, and Exercise

Diana Bogueva[a] *and Dora Marinova*[b]

[a]University of Sydney, Australia
[b]Curtin University of Technology, Australia

Abstract

Many in Generation Z are concerned about health, nutrition, and lifestyle. They are sensitive to the social determinants of health, represented through concerns about access to health care, viable and affordable housing, poverty, and unemployment. They are also concerned about food choices, their environmental footprint, and the way food is produced. There is similarly high awareness about the importance of nutrition for health. Despite engaging in physical exercise, Generation Z is also exposed to the risks associated with obesity and sedentary lifestyle.

Keywords: Determinants of health; nutrition; obesity; food; exercise; fitness

After the first five years of life, the burden of disease drops significantly (Roser et al., 2021) and remains low until the age of 50 after which the Disability-Adjusted Life Years (DALYs) gradually increase (WHO, 2022). The DALYs measure years of human life lost because of death and time lived in less than full health (WHO, 2022). Generation Z has some of the lowest DALYs due to low morbidity and mortality (Roser et al., 2021). However, given the changes in lifestyle, nutrition patterns, and the way food is produced, the future health of today's younger people may be at risk in the longer term. Insufficient physical activity among adolescents seems to be looming as a major concern (Guthold et al., 2020). Poor food choices, malnutrition, and obesity are other important factors that can affect Generation Z's current health and future outlook (World Obesity Atlas, 2022).

Health describes the condition of the human body and characterizes the lack or presence of diseases as well as its fitness level and ability to perform. This determines the ability of people to function within society and the economy, their capacity to live, learn, love, work, and play within the environments of the natural, social, and digital worlds (Boczkowski & Mitchelstein, 2021). Health is

Gen Z Around the World, 79–89
Copyright © 2024 Diana Bogueva and Dora Marinova
Published under exclusive licence by Emerald Publishing Limited
doi:10.1108/978-1-83797-092-620241009

extremely important to Generation Z (Linus, 2022). One participant from the Global Gen Z Study said: "I worry the most about being able to survive. . . I fear I will not be able to support myself in a way that allows me to stay physically healthy and pursue the intellectual and cultural actions that make me feel whole and thus support my mental health."

Social Determinants of Health

Since the early 2000s, significant evidence emerged internationally that individual and population health is strongly influenced by nonmedical factors related to the socioeconomic environments where people live (Commission of the Social Determinants of Health, 2008). These factors described as social determinant of health (Baum, 2016) represent inequalities in the conditions where people are born and live. The circumstances of their daily lives, such as income and housing, impact on the ability to access health care when needed, or obtain the desired level of education. Table 9.1 includes the percentage of Gen Zers from the Global Gen Z Study who indicate being concerned or very concerned about each social determinant.

Access to Health Care

Although the health risk factors for young people are relatively lower based on the DALY measurements, maintaining good health translates into opportunities to achieve better educational outcomes, transition to employment, overcome the challenges of parenthood and family life, as well as maintain friendships and lead healthy adult lives (AIHW, 2022). Availability and accessibility of health-care services contribute to these opportunities, and they can assist with health challenges.

For one, preventative health care can include immunization and vaccination initiatives, family planning and sexual reproduction educational programs, campaigns against smoking and substance abuse, as well as regular check-ups. In addition, dental services, medical tests, specialized treatment, and physiotherapy can all contribute to preventative health care.

New technologies, such as telehealth, digitalization, and more accurate diagnostics equipment, are constantly introduced, improving the level of medical care (Shen et al., 2021). These technologies, though, also push up medical costs, which

Table 9.1. Social Determinants of Health.

Social Determinant	Percent Concerned or Very Concerned
Access to health care	63%
Poverty	63%
Access to viable and affordable housing	62%
Unemployment	53%

can result in challenges in accessing health care and availability of services particularly in poor, remote, and vulnerable communities.

The Global Gen Z Survey indicates a very high level of concern about access to health care. Table 9.2 outlines levels of concern globally and by regions with highest and lowest percentages.

Access to health care appeared among the top 10 social concerns globally – third after racism and education. High levels of concern varied, however, being less of a concern in regions where there are substantial levels of socialized health care.

Poverty

Poverty may affect Generation Z's attitude toward health and nutrition as limited access to healthy food choices impacts health (Centers for Disease Control, 2020). In addition, poverty can contribute to health inequalities within countries as is often the case between Indigenous and non-Indigenous populations (Marmot, 2011). Table 9.3 highlights concern for poverty across all global regions as well as those with the highest and lowest levels.

While poverty is a concern for many, there are regional differences. For example, the Africa and Latin America regions had the highest rates of concern, which makes sense given that the vast majority of the poorest countries in the world are situated in Africa and Latin America (World Population Review, 2023). In addition, this high level of concern may be attributed to individual fears for Gen Zers' own future or represent a broader societal concern; nevertheless, it shows that inadequate income and insufficient means to lead a normal life are worries of young people.

While poverty was a global concern, fewer Gen Zers in the Confucian region and in Protestant Europe indicated being concerned or highly concerned. This may be related to their own personal circumstances or the lower poverty ranking overall of the countries they represent (World Population Review, 2023).

Access to Viable and Affordable Housing

Access to viable and affordable housing is another social determinant of health (Rolfe et al., 2020), which involves having a secure and comfortable home

Table 9.2. Access to Health Care.

	Global	Regions With Highest Levels of Concern	Regions With Lowest Levels of Concern
Concerned or very concerned	63%	Latin America (88%) Africa[a] (86%)	Protestant Europe (40%) Confucian (40%)

[a]Not included in the World Values Survey.

Table 9.3. Poverty.

	Global	Regions With Highest Levels of Concern	Regions With Lowest Levels of Concern
Concerned or very concerned	63%	Africa[a] (87%) Latin America (85%)	Confucian (38%) Protestant Europe (49%)

[a]Not included in the World Values Survey.

environment. Viable and affordable housing substantially affects physical and mental health and overall sense of well-being. The quality of the neighborhood and local social support also impact people (Rolfe et al., 2020). Furthermore, the affordability and stability of the housing arrangements influence, be it indirectly, human health (Hernandez & Suglia, 2016).

The high cost of housing can prevent younger people, in particular, from accessing secure and safe housing options, leading to negative health impacts. By comparison, housing policies that ensure affordable access as well as public housing can help with mental health issues (Mwoka et al., 2021). Young people are a key vulnerable population for accessing adequate housing, particularly in a political framework that sees housing as a commodity rather than an element of human development, health, and wellness (Mwoka et al., 2021).

Globally, 62% of Gen Zers are very concerned or concerned about viable and affordable housing. Table 9.4 outlines global rates, along with the regions with the highest and lowest levels of concern.

In looking at the data by region, Gen Zers from Africa and Latin America expressed the highest number of those who were concerned or highly concerned. While Orthodox Europe had the second lowest rates of concern, those rates were still considerably higher than the Confucian region with the lowest. Given that every other region in the world had a majority who indicated being concerned or highly concerned, it is likely that this is a more similar sentiment than the Confucian outlier may indicate, which may be explained by its placement as a

Table 9.4. Access to Viable and Affordable Housing.

	Global	Regions With Highest Levels of Concern	Regions With Lowest Levels of Concern
Concerned or very concerned	62%	Africa[a] (87%) West and South Asia (80%)	Confucian (21%) Orthodox Europe (51%)

[a]Not included in the World Values Survey.

region with lower poverty rankings (World Population Review, 2023). Further, while poverty is often a societal indicator, access to housing may be a more personal one. Given the financial concerns of many in Generation Z worldwide, it makes sense that individuals may find securing adequate housing to be particularly difficult with their limited incomes.

Unemployment

Not only are there differences in available economic and social resources between those who are employed and those who are not, which leads to a health gap, but the lack of trust in the institutional system designed to offer support, particularly for young and vulnerable population groups is a contributing factor to that very health gap (Brydsten et al., 2018). Some describe income and wealth as the "cause of the causes" in the social determinants of health (Braveman & Gottlieb, 2014).

Fifty-three percent of Gen Zers expressed being very concerned or concerned about unemployment. Table 9.5 outlines the levels of concern at the global and highest and lowest regional levels.

Unemployment did not appear in the top 10 concerns globally or in any of the regions. A possible explanation of why this issue ranked lower than others may be due to the nature of the sample of the study participants as only 24% of the participants' households had income below the average and almost all were university students predominantly studying full time.

At the regional level, again Africa and Latin America indicated the highest numbers for those being concerned or very concerned about unemployment. The lowest were the Confucian region and Protestant Europe. These findings appear to be consistent with those of the other social determinants of health and supported by their poverty rankings (World Population Review, 2023).

Despite the overall positive outlook for the future of the Global Gen Z given their high education studies, the results show that when it comes to physical health, the global Gen Z cohort, at large, are concerned about the factors that contribute to the social determinants of health.

Table 9.5. Unemployment.

	Global	Regions With Highest Levels of Concern	Regions With Lowest Levels of Concern
Concerned or very concerned	53%	Africa[a] (87%) Latin America (84%)	Confucian (24%) Protestant Europe (29%)

[a]Not included in the World Values Survey.

Commercial Determinants

In addition to the social determinants of health, commercial interests also impact population health (Maani et al., 2022). These commercial determinants of health manifest themselves by putting profits, along with socially and environmentally irresponsible practices, above the physical well-being of people and the planet. In a competitive market economy, government policies rarely manage to safeguard the public from the harmful impacts of commercial products (World Obesity Atlas, 2022). Nutrition, food production, healthy food options, and obesity are some of the key commercial determinants of health.

Nutrition

The connection between health and human diet has become not just an environmental, social, and cultural issue with Generation Z, but also a political and public policy issue (Carnegie, 2022). This issue is projected to be a disruptor to existing food systems and the food industry globally (Marinova & Bogueva, 2022). The food preferences of Generation Z will shape the development of many new products and their dietary choices will be made with greater environmental awareness compared to previous generations. Gen Zers are more concerned than the previous generations about the environmental impacts of their food choices and take a more holistic approach to health and nutrition (International Food Information Council, 2022). Plant-based offerings are increasingly popular with them as is the presentability of food (McLymont, 2022). In addition to eating more plant-based foods, they are also slated to be active participants in a sustainability transition toward more plant-based food choices (Marinova et al., 2022).

Food Production

Generation Z's desire for transparency in the way food is produced is combined with awareness about the health benefits of fresh and wholesome food. Seventy eight percent of those in Generation Z want more transparency related to food production from government as well as food brands (EIT, 2021). Factory farming, that is raising farm animals intensively in densely populated environments (Anomaly, 2015), reduces the cost of animal-based foods but poses public health risks, including easy spread of viruses and diseases. These practices are also associated with cruelty toward animals (Huemer, 2019). A 2021 Australian study highlights that two-thirds of those in Generation Z are concerned about animal cruelty (Year13, 2021).

The data from the Global Gen Z Survey indicates 48% are very concerned or concerned about factory farming/unhealthy food production. Despite the number who are concerned, this issue did not appear among the top 10 concerns globally or regionally. Table 9.6 showcases the global data with the regions with the highest and lowest levels of concern.

Table 9.6. Factory Farming/Unhealthy Food Production.

	Global	Regions With Highest Levels of Concern	Regions With Lowest Levels of Concern
Concerned or very concerned	48%	Protestant Europe (63%) Africa[a] (57%)	West and South Asia (28%) Confucian (32%)

[a]Not included in the World Values Survey.

While the rates of concern for Protestant Europe and Africa, which were the two highest, weren't considerably higher than the mean, the lower levels in the two Asian regions could be informative. A study by McKinsey & Company found that Gen Zers in Asia support sustainability and environmental consciousness; however many don't want to pay more for sustainably sourced products (Kim et al., 2020). Perhaps their moderate levels of concern are symbiotic with their willingness to spend on environmentally conscious food.

In addition, the lower level of concern globally compared to other issues, however, doesn't mean this issue isn't on the minds of Gen Zers, especially since only 11% of the global participants indicated not being concerned at all about it. Perhaps other issues are more on the radar of young people given the attention paid to them by policymakers, their prevalence in news stories, and the social movements that many in Generation Z are already involved in around social justice and climate change (Carnegie, 2022).

Healthy Food Options

This generation is also knowledgeable about health and nutrition. Research conducted among Generation Z in Europe shows that young people consider healthy eating to be critical to both physical and mental health (EIT, 2021). Seven in 10 prefer healthy food options while eating at home and overall, nearly three-quarters see good nutrition contributing to them staying healthy.

Commercial actors who stand to gain a profit may encourage poor nutritional choices in order to sell their products. These food producers and retailers make and sell food and drinks that are ultra-processed, high in sugar content, fatty, and/or low in nutrients and fiber but high in calories. The ad campaigns and catchy slogans have the ability to draw in consumers, which is why it isn't surprising that 40% of Gen Zers consume at least one energy or sports drink per week (YouGov, 2022). While that number is lower than the 50% of Millennials who do, it is considerably higher than that of older generations, indicating the target market for these types of drinks being younger people. If left unchecked and unregulated, the commercial determinants of health will continue to shape both the health and economic systems in which Generation Z will have to contend with.

Obesity

The World Obesity Atlas (2022) estimates that by 2030, one billion people worldwide will be living with obesity – one in five women and one in seven men. Obesity is classified as a multifactorial disease with serious consequences (World Obesity Federation, 2021), such as diabetes type 2, cardiovascular disease, cancer, and hypertension. Alarmingly, the number of people of young age who are obese is increasing with childhood and adolescent obesity at historic highs and projections to grow (World Obesity Atlas, 2022).

Health systems are ill-prepared to deal with the consequences from obesity and overweight (World Obesity Atlas, 2022), with economic costs measuring in the billions of dollars that not all economies can afford. While obesity is a health issue, it will likely be a costly economic issue for those in Generation Z who will be left to make policy decisions after older generations have passed.

Exercise

In addition to social and commercial determinants of health having affected Gen Zers' life choices when it comes to physical wellness, so do their exercise preferences and behaviors.

Sedentary Versus Active Lifestyle

For one, Gen Zers' physical health is impacted by a sedentary lifestyle (Sparks & Honey, 2014), which can be linked to intensive use of electronic devices, social media and gaming, limited physical exercise, and lack of regular medical and preventative checkups. One-third of people worldwide who are over the age of 15 engage in insufficient physical activities; this sedentary behavior has wide-ranging adverse impacts on the body (Park et al., 2020). Young people are particularly exposed to the risks associated with sedentary lifestyle making some commentators call them "Generation Z(edentary)" (Lawrence, 2017).

Many in Generation Z, however, report engaging in high levels of physical exercise, with 49% indicating that they work out one to three times per week (AdAge, 2018), which is above average compared to the general population. However, in looking specifically at the United States, Gen Zers have the lowest percentage of participation rates in fitness sports (56%) compared to Baby Boomers and Gen Xers at 64% and Millennials at 70% (Statista, 2022). While they may have higher rates than other generations in terms of engaging in physical exercise in general, their choice of workout is not necessarily fitness sports. Home gyms, jogging, weight lifting, strength training, pilates, yoga, aerobic, and cardio exercising are all popular ways that Gen Zers report maintaining health and wellness (Commisso, 2022).

Motivators for Fitness

Gen Zers' preferences and behaviors in other areas of their lives may be informative when it comes to understanding what might work as motivators for fitness. A study by IHRSA, a global health and fitness association, found that gym use has been declining among Gen Zers since the COVID-19 pandemic (2022). However, 42% of Gen Zers own a wearable fitness tracker (Commisso, 2022), the desire to set goals, track, and monitor their fitness appears to be important to them, which aligns with this cohort being motivated by accomplishment and milestones. Wearable fitness devices provide elements of gamification and badging that aims to gamify fitness. While there has been a decline in gym memberships, Gen Zers' strong usage of these devices may point to a generation that is choosing to exercise outside of formal fitness centers.

Conclusion

Generation Z has already embraced a wide range of social issues related to human well-being and social determinants of health, and many Gen Zers are concerned about unhealthy food production. However, there is a range of other significant issues such as commercial determinants of health that include obesity and sedentary lifestyles that they will need to tackle, both for themselves and for society at large. In many ways, Generation Z is more aware of the environmental implications of its food choices and is already opting for more plant-based options. While food is a personal choice, more efforts are needed by policymakers and society at large to reduce the social and commercial determinants of health and decrease the vulnerability of young people when it comes to housing, access to health care, poverty, and unemployment. The food industry will similarly have to respond to the expectations about transparency and improved nutritional quality. There is also a role for educators, parents, and supervisors to encourage active lifestyles and reduce alarming obesity trends to achieve better health and well-being outcomes for Generation Z, particularly capitalizing on Gen Zers' preferences for exercise and fitness.

References

AdAge. (2018). *Z: A generation redefining health and wellness.* https://cdn2.hubspot.net/hubfs/4000540/content-reports/reports-pdf-versions/UNiDAYS-Ad-Age-Health-Wellness-2018-Report.pdf

Anomaly, J. (2015). What's wrong with factory farming? *Public Health Ethics, 8*(3), 246–254. https://doi.org/10.1093/phe/phu001

Australian Institute of Health and Welfare (AIHW). (2022). *Health of young people.* https://www.aihw.gov.au/reports/children-youth/health-of-young-people

Baum, F. (2016). *The new public health* (4th ed.). Oxford University Press.

Boczkowski, P. J., & Mitchelstein, A. (2021). *The digital environment: How we live, learn, work, and play now.* MIT Press.

Braveman, P., & Gottlieb, L. (2014). The social determinants of health: It's time to consider the causes of the causes. *Public Health Reports, 129*(Suppl. 2), 19–31. https://doi.org/10.1177/00333549141291S206

Brydsten, A., Hammarström, A., & San Sebastian, M. (2018). Health inequalities between employed and unemployed in northern Sweden: A decomposition analysis of social determinants for mental health. *International Journal for Equity in Health, 17*, 59. https://doi.org/10.1186/s12939-018-0773-5

Carnegie, M. (2022). Gen Z: How young people are changing activism. https://www.bbc.com/worklife/article/20220803-gen-z-how-young-people-are-changing-activism

Centers for Disease Control. (2020). *Healthy food environments: Improving access to healthier food.* https://www.cdc.gov/nutrition/healthy-food-environments/improving-access-to-healthier-food.html

Commission of the Social Determinants of Health. (2008). *Closing the gap in a generation: Health equity through action on the social determinants of health – Final report of the commission on social determinants of health.* https://www.who.int/publications/i/item/WHO-IER-CSDH-08.1

Commisso, D. (2022). *7 quick health & fitness trends that lead among Gen Z.* https://civicscience.com/7-quick-health-fitness-trends-that-lead-among-gen-z/#:~:text=Gen%20Z%20is%20big%20into,compared%20to%20the%20general%20population

European Institute of Innovation and Technology (EIT) Food. (2021). *Our food, our food system: What Generation Z wants from a healthy food system.* https://www.eitfood.eu/media/news-pdf/Our_Food,_Our_Food_System_-_EIT_Food_report_.pdf

Guthold, R., Stevens, G. A., Riley, L. M., & Bull, F. C. (2020). Global trends in insufficient physical activity among adolescents: A pooled analysis of 298 population-based surveys with 1.6 million participants. *The Lancet Child & Adolescent Health, 4*(1), 23–35. https://doi.org/10.1016/S2352-4642(19)30323-2

Hernandez, D., & Suglia, S. (2016). *Housing as a social determinant of health.* Columbia University. https://healthequity.globalpolicysolutions.org/wp-content/uploads/2016/12/Housing2.pdf

Huemer, M. (2019). *Dialogues on ethical vegetarianism.* Routledge.

IHRSA. (2022). *COVID and the next generation of fitness consumers.* https://www.ihrsa.org/improve-your-club/covid-and-the-next-generation-of-fitness-consumers/#:~:text=Fewer%20Gen%20Z%27s%20are%20exercising%20weekly%20than%20pre%2Dpandemic.&text=Exercise%20decreased%20to%2058%25%20in,adults%20dropping%20their%20exercise%20habits

International Food Information Council. (2022). *2022 Food and health survey.* https://foodinsight.org/wp-content/uploads/2022/05/IFIC-2022-Food-and-Health-Survey-Report.pdf

Kim, A., McInerney, P., Rüdiger Smith, T., & Yamakawa, N. (2020). *What makes Asia – Pacific's Generation Z different?* https://www.mckinsey.com/capabilities/growth-marketing-and-sales/our-insights/what-makes-asia-pacifics-generation-z-different#/auth-download/%2F~%2Fmedia%2Fmckinsey%2Fbusiness%20functions%2Fmarketing%20and%20sales%2Four%20insights%2Fwhat%20makes%20asia%20pacifics%20generation%20z%20different%2Fwhat-makes-asia-pacifics-generation-z-different.pdf

Lawrence, C. (2017). *Generation Z(edentary).* https://www.linkedin.com/pulse/generation-zedentary-case-lawrence/

Linus. (2022). *Gen Z + the future of health*. https://www.thelinusgroup.com/gen-z-report

Maani, M., Petticrew, M., & Galea, S. (Eds.). (2022). *The commercial determinants of health*. Oxford University Press.

Marinova, D., & Bogueva, D. (2022). *Food in a planetary emergency*. Springer.

Marinova, D., Bogueva, D., Wu, Y., & Guo, X. (2022). China and changing food trends: A sustainability transition perspective. *Ukrainian Food Journal*, *11*(1), 126–147. https://doi.org/10.24263/2304-974X-2022-11-1-13

Marmot, M. (2011). Social determinants and the health of Indigenous Australians. *Medical Journal of Australia*, *194*(10), 512–513. https://doi.org/10.5694/j.1326-5377.2011.tb03086.x

McLymont, V. (2022). *What Gen Z wants: A look inside their food preferences*. https://hospitalitynewsny.com/what-gen-z-wants-a-look-inside-their-food-preferences/

Mwoka, M., Biermann, O., Ettman, C. K., Abdalla, S. M., Ambuko, J., Pearson, M., Rashid, S. F., Zeinali, Z., Galea, S., Valladares, L. M., & Mberu, B. (2021). Housing as a social determinant of health: Evidence from Singapore, the UK, and Kenya: The 3-D Commission. *Journal of Urban Health*, *98*(Suppl. 1), 15–30. https://doi.org/10.1007/s11524-021-00557-8

Park, J. H., Moon, J. H., Kim, H. J., Kong, M. H., & Oh, Y. H. (2020). Sedentary lifestyle: Overview of updated evidence of potential health risks. *Korean Journal of Family Medicine*, *41*(6), 365–373. https://doi.org/10.4082/kjfm.20.0165

Rolfe, S., Garnham, L., Godwin, J., Anderson, I., Seaman, P., & Donaldson, C. (2020). Housing as a social determinant of health and wellbeing: Developing an empirically-informed realist theoretical framework. *BMC Public Health*, *20*, 1138. https://doi.org/10.1186/s12889-020-09224-0

Roser, M., Ritchie, H., & Spooner, S. (2021). *Burden of disease*. https://ourworldindata.org/burden-of-disease

Shen, Y.-T., Chen, L., Yue, W.-W., & Xu, H.-X. (2021). Digital technology-based telemedicine for the COVID-19 pandemic. *Frontiers in Medicine*, *8*, 646506. https://doi.org/10.3389/fmed.2021.646506

Sparks & Honey. (2014). *Meet Generation Z: Forget everything you learned about Millennials*. https://www.slideshare.net/sparksandhoney/generation-z-final-june-17

Statista. (2022). *Participation rate in fitness sports in the United States in 2021, by age group*. https://www.statista.com/statistics/1051774/us-participation-in-fitness-sports-by-generation/

World Health Organization (WHO). (2022). *Disability-adjusted life years (DALYs)*. https://www.who.int/data/gho/indicator-metadata-registry/imr-details/158

World Obesity Atlas. (2022). *World Obesity Atlas 2022*. https://www.worldobesity.org/resources/resource-library/world-obesity-atlas-2022

World Obesity Federation. (2021). *Obesity is a disease*. https://www.worldobesityday.org/assets/downloads/Obesity_Is_a_Disease.pdf

World Population Review. (2023). *Poverty rate by country 2023*. https://worldpopulationreview.com/country-rankings/poverty-rate-by-country

Year13. (2021). Gen Z's animal cruelty awakening. https://year13.com.au/business/articles/gen-zs-animal-cruelty-awakening?next=gen-zs-animal-cruelty-awakening

YouGov. (2022). *US: Pepsico announces deal with Celsius Holdings – Who exactly consumes energy drinks regularly?* https://business.yougov.com/content/43454-us-pepsico-announces-deal-celsius-holdings-who-exa

Chapter 10

Parameters of Well-being

Radka Massaldjieva and Mariya Karaivanova

Medical University of Plovdiv, Bulgaria

Abstract

The importance of well-being at all ages is well-argued theoretically and experimentally, with it having a special place during adolescence and young adulthood, largely because of its association with mental health. Thus, it is important to better understand influences affecting the well-being of Generation Z and explore plans for adequate interventions. In addition, with factors pointing to high psychological well-being among Gen Zers, there are grounds for positive expectations for this generation. This can help optimize programs to improve mental health at a young age, which has important implications for the whole life spectrum.

Keywords: Well-being; mental health; personal growth; social inclusion; psychological well-being; flourishing and languishing

Well-being and positive mental health have been the subject of research in philosophy, psychology, epidemiology, and social sciences (Huppert, 2009; Tiberius, 2006). Positive emotions, self-confidence, social contribution, and coping with difficulties are part of the World Health Organization's (WHO) definition of mental health (2001). A high level of well-being is considered synonymous with positive mental health and is associated with emotional stability, optimism, competence, engagement, meaning, and positive relationships (Huppert & So, 2013).

The importance of well-being at all ages is well-argued theoretically and experimentally, with it having a special place during adolescence and young adulthood, largely because of its association with mental health problems, which are a significant factor in impaired functioning in childhood and adolescence. Seventy-five percent of all mental illnesses begin by age 24 (Parekh, 2015), and they are among the most significant child and adolescent health burdens (Otto et al., 2021). Of those in the Global Gen Z Study who indicated having a disability, 54% indicated having a psychological disability (20 % of all

Gen Z Around the World, 91–99

Copyright © 2024 Radka Massaldjieva and Mariya Karaivanova

Published under exclusive licence by Emerald Publishing Limited

doi:10.1108/978-1-83797-092-620241010

participants). This is a larger percentage than the WHO's (2022) estimates for the entire global population at about 12.5%.

Mental health issues can increase vulnerability to physical illness, and when it occurs in childhood and is not resolved successfully, it can increase the risks of emotional problems or related illnesses during adulthood (Ruggeri et al., 2020; Stewart-Brown, 1998). In an 11-year longitudinal study in children and adolescents in Germany, impaired mental health has been a predictor of future general and mental health issues (Otto et al., 2021). Further, suicide mortality is a significant consideration, especially with higher rates of suicide among young people in both low-income and middle-income countries (Ghebreyesus, 2019). It's not surprising then that mental and emotional well-being is among the seven priority areas for the US National Prevention Strategy, based on the relationship between emotional well-being and public health (Feller et al., 2018).

As a result of an important change at the end of the last century, which opened the horizon to the study of positive mental health and well-being rather than of mental disorders, mental well-being is presented as a continuum from languishing, which involves feelings of emptiness or even despair, to flourishing, which involves feelings of general enthusiasm (Huppert, 2009). While individuals who languish or flourish can have mental health issues, those who are more toward the languishing end of the continuum are at higher risk for depression specifically (Huppert, 2009). Thus, intervention to help individuals move toward flourishing may have utility in preventing mental health issues.

Many studies have been conducted based on different conceptions of the limits and structure of well-being (e.g., Bradburn, 1969; Diener et al., 1999; Ryff, 1989) as a composite construct having several different dimensions and components (Ruggeri et al., 2020). Three areas of well-being can be summarized as:

- Subjective or hedonic well-being, which covers affective and cognitive aspects (emotions, moods, and life satisfaction) (Diener et al., 1999).
- Psychological or eudaimonic well-being with confirmed six dimensions – autonomy, environmental mastery, personal growth, positive relations with others, purpose in life, and self-acceptance (Ryff & Keyes, 1995).
- Social well-being, which involves individual interpersonal functioning (Keyes, 1998).

The parameters of Generation Z's well-being include perceptions of the future and expectations (subjective), striving for personal growth and positive relations with others (psychological), and social inclusion and commitment to worthwhile causes and social problems (social).

Subjective Well-being

One element of subjective well-being involves one's outlook, whether more optimistic or pessimistic. Not surprisingly, a positive relationship has been found between optimism and well-being (Augusto-Landa et al., 2011) as well as helping one effectively cope with stress (Jiménez et al., 2017). Understanding the extent to which Gen Zers are optimistic may have a role in their subjective well-being.

Before the COVID-19 pandemic, Seemiller and Grace (2016) found a predominance of optimism with 60% of American college students from Generation Z being optimistic about the future. Findings from the Global Gen Z Study, which included Gen Zers from countries around the world and conducted during the pandemic, indicated that only 38% are optimistic about the future. In looking at the qualitative data from the study, many are worried about the future. For example, one Gen Zer said, "[I worry] that I am making the wrong choices, and that my life will not be as good as it could be." Another held a more macro view in saying, "[I worry] that the future is bleak no matter how drastic a change in course humanity takes."

Positive mental health is an irrevocable condition for achieving successful realization of abilities in work and in other spheres of social life (National Prevention Council, 2011), which may be related to outlook. For instance, the Gen Zers in the Global Gen Z study who reported having no psychological disability had a higher mean composite score for optimism compared to the group having some form of psychological disability. Further, significantly more participants with a psychological disability "plan for the worst case scenario" compared to those reporting no psychological disability. Previous research has found a link between optimism and mental health, whereas a positive outlook can help both promote a healthy lifestyle and contribute to more effective coping strategies, particularly around adaptability, flexibility, and problem-solving (Conversano et al., 2010). Optimism is positively related to physical and mental health and at the same time, there are few studies on Generation Z and optimism (Biber et al., 2022).

Psychological Well-being

Striving for personal growth and positive relations with others are two of the components of psychological (eudaimonic) well-being as conceptualized by Ryff (1989). In looking at motivators from the Global Gen Z Study, results show a strong desire for personal growth. This is consistent with existing data on Gen Z describing them as competitive, focused, and entrepreneurial (Biber et al., 2022). Table 10.1 showcases the percentage of Gen Zers who are greatly motivated by each of the motivators listed.

Significant cultural differences in the level of well-being have been found (Huppert & So, 2013), and this calls for comparative studies between regions. In looking at psychological well-being-related motivators by World Values Regions (World Values Survey Association, 2022), personal growth motivators are the highest for Gen Zers primarily from Latin America, Africa, and African-Islamic countries. These higher percentages might be explained after considering economic factors in particular geographic regions. Higher rates of poverty in many countries in Latin America and Africa (World Population Review, 2023) might fuel a strong desire for Gen Zers to learn, take advantage of new opportunities,

Table 10.1. Personal Growth Motivators Related to Psychological Well-being.

Sources of Motivation	Global	Regions With Lowest Percentages	Regions With Highest Percentages
Seeing the fruits of your labor/ accomplishment	71%	Confucian (52%) English-Speaking (61%)	Africa[a] (83%) Latin America (82%)
Having an opportunity for advancement (promotion, new opportunities)	66%	Protestant Europe (46%) Confucian (57%)	Latin America (81%) African-Islamic (77%)
Learning something or being better at something	65%	Confucian (37%) English-Speaking (57%)	Latin America (74%) African-Islamic (73%)
Gaining experience to build your resume	55%	Protestant Europe (43%) Confucian (45%)	African-Islamic (68%) Africa (67%) Latin America (67%)

[a]Not included in the World Values Survey.

and use the satisfaction of achievements as an ongoing incentive for self-improvement. Research supports this notion in that Gil-Hernández and Gracia (2018) reported higher college aspirations of African and Latin American migrant students in Spain compared to students of Spanish origin.

In terms of positive relations with others, Table 10.2 showcases the percentage of Gen Zers who are greatly motivated by each of the motivators.

Cultural influences affect not only behavior but also perceptions and ideas about relationships (Lalonde et al., 2004). In this sense, it is possible that the essential importance of good relations with others reflects cultural differences. For instance, in the Confucian region, being motivated because of a desire to impact others is not as essential, whereas it is more so for other regions of the world.

Social Well-being

Social well-being is described and measured through components such as social integration, which can include social adjustment and social support (Larson, 1993), social contribution, social coherence, social actualization, and social acceptance (Keyes, 1998). Individuals are integrated in society and socially

Table 10.2. Positive Relations Motivators Related to Psychological Well-being.

Sources of Motivation	Global	Regions With Lowest Percentages	Regions With Highest Percentages
Not wanting to let others down	63%	Africa[a] (38%) Confucian (42%)	West and South Asia (74%) English-Speaking (72%)
Pleasing others (impress or appease family or friends)	45%	Confucian (20%) Orthodox Europe (20%)	Protestant Europe (71%) Catholic Europe (52%)
Making a difference for someone else	59%	Confucian (27%) Orthodox Europe (46%)	Africa (75%) West and South Asia (72%)

[a]Not included in the World Values Survey.

adjusted if they are involved in activities related to different social structures through participation in social roles and networks (Larson, 1993; Song, 2013).

In looking at the Global Gen Z Study, several factors may contribute to Gen Zers' social well-being. For instance, 75% like group work; 42% enjoy social learning, and 39% enjoy interpersonal learning (the highest two modalities for enjoyment); and, 77% like face-to-face communication. In addition, 57% volunteered during the last year. Research has found that volunteering can lead to higher social capital, greater emotional support, and a decrease in social isolation (Healthy People 2030, 2023), all factors that can contribute to social well-being. Further, 57% of Gen Zers in the Global Gen Z Study indicated working 20 or more hours per week. Ivanov et al. (2020) compared unemployed with working individuals and found greater risk of psychopathology (depression, suicide, and alcohol abuse) in unemployed subjects. Thus, employment may help increase social well-being (Ivanov et al., 2020). Working and being around others, through settings such as school and group activities, serve as important factors for social well-being.

Indicators of Well-being

Based on findings from the Global Gen Z Study, there appears to be a relationship between preference for group work and motivators related to personal growth and positive relations. For example, a higher percentage, generally, of

Table 10.3. Motivators and Group Work Preference.

Sources of Motivation	Percentage of Those Who Like Working in Groups	Percentage of Those Who Do Not Like Working in Groups
Seeing the fruits of your labor/accomplishment	73%	65%
Having an opportunity for advancement (promotion, new opportunities)	69%	58%
Learning something or being better at something	66%	60%
Gaining experience to build your resume	58%	44%
Not wanting to let others down	64%	61%
Pleasing others (impress or appease family or friends)	45%	45%
Making a difference for someone else	60%	55%

Gen Zers who like working in groups are motivated by the aforementioned personal growth and positive relations motivators compared to those who do not like working in groups. The findings are outlined in Table 10.3.

It is clear – those who enjoy interacting with others indicate being more motivated by various forms of personal growth and positive relations.

Conclusion

There are several trends regarding well-being and Generation Z, some of which might be areas of concern, whereas others might be opportunities for hope. In terms of concerns, there is a high frequency of psychological disabilities (in about a fifth of the participants in the Global Gen Z Study), which requires an analysis of the causes and plans for adequate prevention initiatives and interventions. Second, Gen Zers possess a low level of optimism about the future, and, thus, a propensity for a low level of subjective well-being. It may be important then to help young people develop optimistic outlooks. This can be done by helping Gen Zers build self-confidence so they can feel more self-assured in any given situation as well as resilience for combatting obstacles and mishaps that may emerge. Being self-confident and resilient may help them alleviate, or at least mitigate, the fear of failure as well as reduce or eliminate worrying about not being able to persist through setback. Consider offering workshops, trainings, and skill development sessions for Gen Zers to develop these and other competencies that may contribute to enhancing optimism.

On a more proactive note, the higher level of motivation by personal growth and positive relationships with others give ground for psychological well-being. Tapping into motivators related to personal growth and positive relations may serve an as enhancement for fostering psychological well-being, particularly if many Gen Zers are already motivated by those factors. And, for those who enjoy groups, those levels of motivation are even higher. Being able to help young people develop skills to work better in groups and give them opportunities to do so might be a portal to increasing their motivations that are associated with psychological well-being.

In addition, their favorability toward working in groups, propensity to work in a job, and engagement in volunteer work can foster opportunities to achieve social well-being. However, social well-being could be enhanced through providing more opportunities, in general, for social connection in any setting.

While each form of well-being is significant, they can be interrelated. For example, in a cross-sectional study of students from Indonesia, subjective well-being was strongly and positively correlated with psychological well-being (Pello et al., 2018). So, enhancing one element of well-being could have a positive effect on another.

Having a better understanding of the various dimensions of well-being may help those in older generations curb mental health and well-being issues among Gen Zers while at the same time garner support and resources to address these concerns more globally (Coverdale & Long, 2015).

References

Augusto-Landa, J. M., Pulido-Martos, M., & Lopez-Zafra, E. (2011). Does perceived emotional intelligence and optimism/pessimism predict psychological well-being? *Journal of Happiness Studies, 12*, 463–474. https://doi.org/10.1007/s10902-010-9209-7

Biber, D., Czech, D., Donald, E., Hassett, A. & Tucker, A. (2022). The relationship between sleep duration, BMI and optimism levels in generation Z students. *Journal of Interdisciplinary Studies in Education, 11*(1), 92–101. https://ojed.org/index.php/jise/article/view/3161

Bradburn, N. M. (1969). *The structure of psychological well-being.* Aldine.

Conversano, C., Rotondo, A., Lensi, E., Della Vista, O., Arpone, F., & Reda, M. A. (2010). Optimism and its impact on mental and physical wellbeing. *Clinical Practice and Epidemiology in Mental Health, 6*, 25–29. https://doi.org/10.2174/1745017901006010025

Coverdale, G. E., & Long, A. F. (2015). Emotional wellbeing and mental health: An exploration into health promotion in young people and families. *Perspectives in Public Health, 135*(1), 27–36. https://doi.org/10.1177/1757913914558080

Diener, E., Suh, E. M., Lucas, R. E., & Smith, H. L. (1999). Subjective well-being: Three decades of progress. *Psychological Bulletin, 125*(2), 276–302. https://doi.org/10.1037/0033-2909.125.2.276

Feller, S., Castillo, E., Greenberg, J., Abascal, P., Van Horn, R., & Wells, K., & University of California, Los Angeles Community Translational Science Team. (2018). Emotional well-being and public health: Proposal for a model national initiative. *Public Health Reports, 133*(2), 136–141.

Ghebreyesus, T. A. (2019). *The WHO special initiative for mental health (2019–2023): Universal health coverage for mental health.* World Health Organization. https://www.jstor.org/stable/resrep28223

Gil-Hernández, C. J., & Gracia, P. (2018). Adolescents' educational aspirations and ethnic background: The case of students of African and Latin American migrant origins in Spain. *Demographic Research, 38,* 577–618.

Healthy People 2030. (2023). *Civic participation.* https://health.gov/healthypeople/priority-areas/social-determinants-health/literature-summaries/civic-participation

Huppert, F. A. (2009). Psychological well-being: Evidence regarding its causes and consequences. *Applied Psychology: Health and Well-being, 1,* 137–164.

Huppert, F. A., & So, T. T. C. (2013). Flourishing across Europe: Application of a new conceptual framework for defining well-being. *Social Indicators Research, 110*(3), 837–861. https://doi.org/10.1007/s11205-011-9966-7

Ivanov, B. F., Pfeiffer, F., & Pohlan, L. (2020). Do job creation schemes improve the social integration and well-being of the long-term unemployed? *Labour Economics, 64,* 101836. https://doi.org/10.1016/j.labeco.2020.101836

Jiménez, M. G., Montorio, I., & Izal, M. (2017). The association of age, sense of control, optimism, and self-esteem with emotional distress. *Developmental Psychology, 53*(7), 1398–1403. https://doi.org/10.1037/dev0000341

Keyes, C. L. M. (1998). Social well-being. *Social Psychology Quarterly, 61,* 121–140.

Lalonde, R. N., Hynie, M., Pannu, M., & Tatla, S. (2004). The role of culture in interpersonal relationships: Do second generation South Asian Canadians want a traditional partner? *Journal of Cross-Cultural Psychology, 35*(5), 503–524.

Larson, J. S. (1993). The measurement of social well-being. *Social Indicators Research, 28,* 285–296.

National Prevention Council. (2011). *National prevention strategy.* https://www.hhs.gov/sites/default/files/disease-prevention-wellness-report.pdf

Otto, C., Reiss, F., Voss, C., Kaman, A., Meyrose, A. K., Hölling, H., & Ravens-Sieberer, U. (2021). Mental health and well-being from childhood to adulthood: Design, methods, and results of the 11-year follow-up of the BELLA study. *European Child & Adolescent Psychiatry, 30.* https://doi.org/10.1007/s00787-020-01630-4

Parekh, R. (2015). *Warning signs of mental illness.* American Psychiatric Association Report. https://www.psychiatry.org/patients-families/warning-signs-of-mental-illness

Pello, S. C., Damayanti, Y., & Benu, J. (2018). Correlation between subjective well-being and psychological well-being among university students. In *4th International Conference on Public Health 2018*, Surakarta, Indonesia (p. 46). Sebelas Maret University. https://doi.org/10.26911/theicph.2018.01.07

Ruggeri, K., Garcia-Garzon, E., Maguire, Á., Matz, S., & Huppert, F. A. (2020). Well-being is more than happiness and life satisfaction: A multidimensional analysis of twenty-one countries. *Health and Quality of Life Outcomes, 18*(1), 192. https://doi.org/10.1186/s12955-020-01423-y

Ryff, C. D. (1989). Happiness is everything, or is it? Explorations on the meaning of psychological well-being. *Journal of Personality and Social Psychology, 57,* 1069–1081.

Ryff, C. D., & Keyes, C. L. M. (1995). The structure of psychological well-being revisited. *Journal of Personality and Social Psychology, 69*(4), 719–727. https://doi.org/10.1037/0022-3514.69.4.719

Seemiller, C., & Grace, M. (2016). *Generation Z goes to college.* Jossey-Bass.

Song, L. (2013). Institutional embeddedness of network embeddedness in the workplace: Social integration at work and employee's health across three societies. *Research in the Sociology of Work, 24,* 323–356.

Stewart-Brown, S. (1998). Emotional wellbeing and its relation to health. *BMJ, 317*(7173), 1608–1609. https://doi.org/10.1136/bmj.317.7173.1608

Tiberius, V. (2006). Well-being: Psychological research for philosophers. *Philosophy Compass, 1,* 493–505. https://doi.org/10.1111/j.1747-9991.2006.00038.x

World Health Organization. (2001). *The world health report—Mental health: New understanding, new hope.* https://apps.who.int/iris/handle/10665/42390

World Health Organization. (2022). *Mental disorders.* https://www.who.int/newsroom/fact-sheets/detail/mental-disorders

World Population Review. (2023). *Poverty rate by country 2023.* https://worldpopulationreview.com/country-rankings/poverty-rate-by-country

World Values Survey Association. (2022). *World values survey.* https://www.worldvaluessurvey.org/WVSContents.jsp

Chapter 11

Financial Literacy and Money Management

Zahrotur Rusyda Hinduan[a] *and Muhamed Irfan Agia*[b]

[a]Universitas Padjadjaran, Indonesia
[b]Bibit Tumbuh Bersama, Indonesia

Abstract

Generation Z continues to face several significant life events that have influenced how they address financial-related problems and manage their money. In addition to worrying about their incomes, access to affordable healthcare and higher education as well as poverty is perceived as the main financial-related issues of concern. COVID-19 might also have strengthened the financial-related awareness of Generation Z, as half of the Global Gen Z Study participants changed spending habits during the pandemic.

Keywords: Income; pandemic; financial concerns; financial literacy; money management; spending habits

The 2008/2009 Great Recession had an impact on many Gen Zers, even those not yet born, as the residual effects of this economic downturn took years to recover from (Seemiller & Grace, 2019). During their childhood, many Gen Zers experienced their parents lose their jobs and struggle to pay their debts; some moved into their grandparents' houses or lived with their extended families (Hinduan et al., 2020).

Just years later, this generation experienced the COVID-19 pandemic. Similar to the Great Recession, this monumental event took place for many Gen Zers during their adolescence. Its impact will also likely persist over their lives since this generation was in the middle of shaping their values during the pandemic. The pandemic brought more financial instability, especially with many layoffs occurring at the onset and during the Delta variant outbreak in mid-2021 (Te'eni-Harari et al., 2022; Valenzuela, 2020). In the Global Gen Z Study, which took place during the height of the pandemic, more than half of Gen Zers indicated being concerned about issues related to the economy. Between the Great

Gen Z Around the World, 101–108

Copyright © 2024 Zahrotur Rusyda Hinduan and Muhamed Irfan Agia

Published under exclusive licence by Emerald Publishing Limited

doi:10.1108/978-1-83797-092-620241011

Recession and the pandemic, it's not surprising that compared to Millennials, Generation Z is perceived as a more realistic generation in terms of economic-related issues (Stillman & Stillman, 2017).

Because of the economic turmoil during the course of their early lives, many want to earn a high salary, and they are willing to work hard to achieve that goal (Dwidienawati & Gandasari, 2018). While income is important for financial stability and security, being financially literate and able to effectively manage money are crucial skills for Gen Zers to have (Stillman & Stillman, 2017).

Financial Literacy

Between people having much more money than they did a generation ago (Pew Research Center, 2018) and the shift in responsibility from employers to employees around pensions for long-term financial planning and retirement (Lusardi, 2019), there will likely be a growing need for young people to be financially literate earlier than previous generations. And, with 57% of Gen Zers in the Global Gen Z Study indicating that they worked 20 or more hours a week, the development of financial literacy and money management skills, especially early in one's lifetime, is essential for financial security.

Financial literacy is defined as the "knowledge and understanding of financial concepts and risks, and the skills, motivation and confidence to apply such knowledge and understanding in order to make effective decisions across a range of financial contexts, to improve the financial well-being of individuals and society, and to enable participation in economic life" (OECD International Network of Financial Education, 2012, p. 13). This kind of literacy includes how an individual seeks financial advice.

A study by Knit (2021) found that Gen Zers need advice and guidance to become financially independent. With the internet being commercialized in 1995, the first year of the Gen Z birth year range, technology has always been at the forefront for those in Generation Z. Many aspects of their lives, including performing daily activities and staying socially connected, depend on technology (Berkup, 2014). So, it makes sense that they currently find a great deal of this advice and guidance online (Knit, 2021). Thirty percent of Gen Zers in the Global Gen Z Study indicated getting information about money and financial matters from social media, which is in line with a study conducted by Banking Rates (2021) that also found 30% learn financial information from social media outlets.

When online, Gen Zers have many options to learn about finances whether through bite-sized content like TikTok, podcasts, visual education like Instagram, and more comprehensive videos like YouTube. According to findings from the Global Gen Z Study, of all platforms, YouTube has the highest Generation Z user rate for learning new information.

Besides learning from social media platforms, 39% of Gen Zers in the Global Gen Z Study engage in learning about finances by accessing online resources like websites, articles, or blogs. However, the abundance of information available could lead to a false sense of security because simply having access to a lot of information does not necessarily equate to having the knowledge and skills needed to make informed financial decisions. Without proper and credible financial education and guidance, Gen Zers may be making decisions based on incomplete or inaccurate information, which could lead to poor financial outcomes.

Further, the quality of the content they are consuming may actually be misinformation since there are few restrictions on who can share online financial education and what they can say. Perhaps out of convenience or accessibility, only 11% of Gen Zers in the Global Gen Z Study sought financial information from people who have a specific and relevant background as a financial professional. With their financial literacy being primarily shaped by social media and online sources, they can access information quickly and easily to make important financial decisions. However, the possibility of the information they gather being inappropriate or inaccurate for their situation could pose a risk.

In addition to basic budgeting and day-to-day financial decision-making, Gen Zers could also benefit from better understanding long-term savings and investment opportunities, especially as they come to realize that their spending and saving habits now will determine their future. While they are keen to save money, few are investing. Findings from the Global Gen Z Study have found that after paying for living expenses, Gen Zers save approximately 24% of their remaining money. However, they only allocate 4% of their remaining money for investing. Since the majority of Gen Zers are young adults may still depend on their parents or guardians financially, they may be drawn more to saving money that can be used anytime rather than investing for the future may feel further down the road. Their economic-related behaviors have likely been shaped by the transfer of learning from their parent's generation who believed that saving in a bank is the safest way to preserve their money (Seemiller & Grace, 2019).

Parents and guardians also play an important role in introducing financial literacy concepts to this generation. In the Global Gen Z Study, most Gen Zers reported that their parents and guardians were the biggest influence on financial matters (84%). With the majority of them looking up to parents and guardians for the "how-to" of financial and money management, parents and guardians must have relevant answers to give them. Many older individuals, though, grew up in an era where certain financial advice may have been recommended given the conditions at the time, in addition to the varied resources now available for people to make important financial decisions. Thus, parental advice based on personal experiences might not be as relevant for future financial challenges for those in Generation Z.

Money Management

On a larger scale, money management includes taking charge of planning and responsibly managing personal finances to achieve financial goals (Munohsamy, 2015). Specifically, this skill involves the "process of controlling income and organizing expenses through a detailed financial plan" (Nigatu, 2.2.1 para 5).

Budgeting, saving, investing, and debt management are also essential for managing financial capital (Munohsamy, 2015).

Financially literacy and money management skills contribute to better financial decision-making, which can result in reduced liabilities and increased assets (Haslem, 2014). Several studies have also shown that financial literacy and money management reflect one's level of conscientiousness and self-determination (Donnelly et al., 2012; Shaner et al., 1999), which can impact individuals' finance-related knowledge as well as their financial goals and motivation. Money management is significantly related to less compulsive buying, increased level of savings, and decreased levels of debt (Donnelly et al., 2012).

Currently, the development in financial technology (fintech) also accelerates financial inclusion and Gen Z is a frontrunner to be the early adopter. There are several apps ranging from money management tools, investment tech, and digital wallets that can help Gen Zers manage their spending and saving behaviors. These technologies give them a hands-on approach to managing their money portfolio. The 2021 study by Knit shows that 43% of Gen Zers use a single platform for all of their financial needs, and nearly two-thirds would do the same if they found one brand that met all of their needs. Further, mobile banking is how 87% of Gen Zers manage their funds.

Financial Implications of the Pandemic

In the early days of the pandemic, many people lost their jobs due to massive shutdowns. It was inevitable that the economic aftermath of the pandemic would result in many of these layoffs being permanent, resulting in greater unemployment rates (OECD, 2020). This situation likely set forth a sentiment for young people that it is necessary to prepare for a volatile job market as employment is not always guaranteed.

It is not surprising then that Gen Zers in the Global Gen Z Study, surveyed during the peak of the pandemic, expressed great concern about issues such as affordable healthcare, poverty/unemployment, and affordable education and housing. These results support previous research conducted by Azimi et al. (2020), which identified the main concerns of this generation during the pandemic being related to health and financial security. These by-products of the pandemic will likely shape Generation Z now and into their future careers.

The pandemic also changed the income spending of this generation. As a result of the pandemic, 52% of Gen Zers in the Global Gen Z Study reported that they changed spending habits. Looking more specifically at their expenses, a study of Millennials when they were in young adulthood found that most spent their spare money on experiences (Schor, 2004). However, based on the findings from the Global Gen Z Study, only 17% of Gen Zers' discretionary income after living expenses was spent on experiences such as travel, holidays, events, and concerts. It is apparent that during the pandemic, Gen Zers closely considered how they spent their money (Gentina, 2020). For example, public events, such as concerts, were limited, and it was difficult for them to travel given the many COVID-19 prevention-related requirements. So, their reduced spending on experiences compared to Millennials when they were the same age may have had more to do with the limited accessibility of experiences versus the necessary day-to-day expenditures that may be more aligned with financial survival during the pandemic.

Although they didn't readily purchase experiences, in the Global Gen Z Study, Gen Zers reported saving 24% of their discretionary income, while spending 24% on nongrocery foods and beverages and 21% on consumer goods. This makes sense in that saving during this critical time may have been at the forefront of their minds, in addition to the fact that they were already predisposed to having a savings mentality before the pandemic (Seemiller & Grace, 2019). As for non-grocery items, during the pandemic, food delivery platforms, such as Uber Eats, became popular since many restaurants were closed. Further, ordering online made it easy to acquire consumer goods.

When disaggregated by World Values Regions (World Values Survey Association, 2022), Table 11.1 shows that nongrocery items, consumer goods, and saving were the three most prominent uses of discretionary funding across all world regions with the exception of Africa, which placed experiences over savings. While the percentage of spending and the order slightly varied between regions, the top three categories were consistent.

After the pandemic, cashless payment becomes more popular among this group of young people. During the stay-at-home order, they bought many things from home using a digital wallet (Hilmi & Pratika, 2021). Thus, this generation is more familiar with those nonconventional payment methods. According to several studies, Gen Zers perceive cashless payment methods as being more convenient and potentially lower risk (Te'eni-Harari et al., 2022).

Along with cashless payment, this generation is interested in using "buy now, pay later" (BNPL) programs, especially when they buy goods or services on e-commerce. While it does involve taking out debt for a purchase, BNPL differs from the use of credit cards or loans as these third-party BNPL programs offer a fixed payment schedule, often selected by the consumer, with far lower interest rates than credit cards. And, those who pay back the amount within four weeks often are able to get the purchase interest free (Lake, 2023). While many in Generation Z may be concerned about financial stability and not want to assume debt, borrowing money out of necessity may be critical if they want to purchase gifts or specialty goods that are needed at a specific time. Many have found out about BNPL from ads or even friends or family members (Backman & Caporal, 2022), whereas the majority have learned about it from social media (Bote, 2022).

Overall, the pandemic's acceleration of the use of digital payment methods among Gen Z may have a lasting impact on their spending habits, as they become more comfortable with digital transactions and seek out more flexible payment options.

Table 11.1. Discretionary Spending by Each Region.

	Experiences	Nongrocery Food and Beverage	Consumer Goods	Invest	Sports Betting or Gambling	Donate to Causes	Give to Friends or Family	Save
Africa[a]	21%	24%	17%	6%	2%	11%	4%	15%
African-Islamic	15%	25%	20%	6%	1%	7%	8%	18%
Catholic Europe	20%	24%	21%	3%	1%	2%	3%	26%
Confucian	14%	25%	27%	2%	1%	3%	8%	20%
English-Speaking	16%	24%	19%	5%	1%	3%	4%	28%
Latin America	13%	24%	20%	7%	1%	4%	7%	25%
Orthodox Europe	18%	26%	22%	3%	1%	3%	8%	18%
Protestant Europe	19%	21%	23%	2%	<1%	2%	3%	29%
West and South Asia	11%	29%	16%	8%	<1%	2%	8%	25%

[a]Not included in the World Values Survey.

Conclusion

Technological advancement and the past financial crisis have shaped their economic-related behaviors. However, the COVID-19 pandemic likely influenced their perspectives regarding their financial behavior. They are aware of the importance of several global financial-social issues, such as access to healthcare, poverty, housing, and education. The spending habits of young people have shifted over time, from buying experiences to buying nongrocery items, consumer goods, and saving for the future. However, they could benefit from informed investment planning and financial education to secure their financial future.

References

Azimi, A. V., Moayed, M. S., Rahimibashar, F., Shojaei, S., Ashtari, S., & Pourhoseingholi, M. A. (2020). Comparison of the severity of psychological distress among four groups of an Iranian population regarding COVID-19 pandemic. *BMC Psychiatry*, *20*(402), 1–7. https://doi.org/10.1186/s12888-020-02804-9

Backman, M., & Caporal, J. (2022). *Study: Buy now, pay later services grow in popularity*. https://www.fool.com/the-ascent/research/buy-now-pay-later-statistics/

Banking Rates. (2021). *Gen Z: The future of finance report*. https://www.gobankingrates.com/gen-z-the-future-of-finances/

Berkup, S. B. (2014). Working with Generations X and Y in Generation Z period: Management of different generations in business life. *Mediterranean Journal of Social Sciences*, *5*(19), 218–229. https://doi.org/10.5901/mjss.2014.v5n19p218

Bote, J. (2022). 'Buy now, pay later' is sending the TikTok generation spiraling into debt, popularized by San Francisco tech firms. *SF Gate*. https://www.sfgate.com/news/article/influencers-lead-Gen-Z-into-debt-17142294.php

Donnelly, G., Iyer, R., & Howell, R. T. (2012). The big five personality traits, materialistic values and financial well-being of self-reported money managers. *Journal of Economic Psychology*, *33*(1), 1129–1142. https://doi.org/10.106/j.joep.2012.08.001

Dwidienawati, D., & Gandasari, D. (2018). Understanding Indonesia's Generation Z. *International Journal of Engineering and Technology (UAE)*, *7*(3), 250–252. https://doi.org/10.14419/ijet.v7i3.25.17556

Gentina, E. (2020). Generation Z in Asia: A research agenda. In E. Gentina & E. Parry (Eds.), *The new Generation Z in Asia: Dynamics, differences, digitalisation* (pp. 3–19). Emerald Publishing Limited.

Haslem, J. A. (2014). Selected topics in financial literacy. *The Journal of Wealth Management*, *17*, 47–57.

Hilmi, L. D., & Pratika, Y. (2021). Paylater feature: Impulsive buying driver for e-commerce in indonesia. *International Journal of Economics, Business and Accounting Research (IJEBAR)*, *5*(2), 63–74.

Hinduan, Z. R., Anggraeni, A., & Agia, M. I. (2020). Generation Z in Indonesia: The self-driven digital. In E. Gentina & E. Parry (Eds.), *The new Generation Z in Asia: Dynamics, differences, digitalisation* (pp. 121–134). Emerald Publishing Limited.

Knit. (2021). *Gen Z's money management (spending, saving, and investment) report 2021.* https://goknit.com/wp-content/uploads/2021/07/Knit-Gen-Z-Money-Management-Report-%E2%80%93-July-2021-July-19-Edition-1.pdf

Lake, R. (2023). *Buy now, pay later vs. credit cards.* https://www.investopedia.com/buy-now-pay-later-vs-credit-cards-5188052

Lusardi, A. (2019). Financial literacy and the need for financial education: Evidence and implications. *Swiss Journal of Economics and Statistics, 1*(155), 1–8. https://doi.org/10.1186/s41937-019-0027-5

Munohsamy, T. (2015). Personal financial management. https://www.activateleadership.co.za/wpcontent/uploads/2021/07/PERSONALFINANCIALMANAGEMENTbyThulasimaniMunohsamy.pdf

Nigatu, S. (2019). *Personal financial management: Which factors affect it?* https://www.grin.com/document/490392

OECD. (2020). *Job retention schemes during the COVID-19 lockdown and beyond.* OECD Policy Responses to Coronavirus (COVID-19). https://www.oecd.org/coronavirus/policy-responses/job-retention-schemes-during-the-covid-19-lockdown-and-beyond-0853ba1d/

OECD International Network of Financial Education. (2012). *PISA 2012 Financial literacy assessment framework.* https://www.oecd.org/pisa/pisaproducts/46962580.pdf

Pew Research Center. (2018). *Young adult households are earning more than most older Americans did at the same age.* https://www.pewresearch.org/fact-tank/2018/12/11/young-adult-households-are-earning-more-than-most-older-americans-did-at-the-same-age/

Schor, J. B. (2004). Understanding the child consumer. *Journal of American Academy of Child and Adolescent Psychiatry, 47*(5), 486–490. https://doi.org/10.1097/CHI.0b013e318167660d

Seemiller, C., & Grace, M. (2019). *Generation Z: A century in the making.* Routledge.

Shaner, A., Tucker, D. E., Roberts, L. J., & Eckman, T. A. (1999). Disability income, cocaine use, and contingency management among patients with cocaine dependence and schizophrenia. In S. T. Higgins & K. Silverman (Eds.), *Motivating behavior change among illicit-drug abusers: Research on contingency management interventions* (pp. 95–121). American Psychological Association.

Stillman, D., & Stillman, J. (2017). *Gen Z@Work: How the next generation is transforming the workplace.* Harper Collins Publisher.

Te'eni-Harari, T., Sela, Y., & Bareket-Bojmel, L. (2022). Gen Z during the COVID-19 crisis: A comparative analysis of the differences between Gen Z and Gen X in resilience, values. *Current Psychology, 1*(1), 1–9. https://doi.org/10.1007/s12144-022-03501-4

Valenzuela, J. (2020). Job loss at home: Children's school performance during the Great Recession. *SERIEs, 11*(3), 243–286. https://doi.org/10.1007/s13209-020-00217-1

World Values Survey Association. (2022). *World values survey.* https://www.worldvaluessurvey.org/WVSContents.jsp

Chapter 12

Career and Entrepreneurship Values and Pursuits

Alfe M. Solina[a], Tamather M. Shatnawi[b],
Liane Vina G. Ocampo[a], Luisa M. Martinez[c]
and Ronalyn I. Garcia[a]

[a]Cavite State University, Philippines
[b]Petra University, Jordan
[c]IPAM Lisboa, Portugal

Abstract

With reduced income and job prospects, many young people are challenged by economic insecurity and struggling to meet their basic needs. In addition, financial stress during the pandemic disrupted many industries, leading to the closure of businesses and downsizing of the workforce. As a result, many Gen Z workers entered their careers during a time in which it was challenging to secure jobs in their desired fields. Despite the circumstances, Gen Zers have clear values related to their professional lives. These include workplace flexibility, financial security, mental well-being, and meaningful work.

Keywords: Job security; employment; workforce; freelancing; career; entrepreneurship

With reduced income and job prospects, many young people are challenged by economic insecurity and struggling to meet their basic needs. The World Economic Forum (2021) has reported that more than half of young people experienced financial stress during the pandemic as it disrupted many industries and led to the closure of businesses and downsizing of the workforce. As a result, many Gen Z workers entered the workforce during a time in which it was challenging to secure jobs in their desired fields. In 2021, Deloitte reported that 44% of Gen Zers globally were worried about finding a job and about the impact of the pandemic on the economy and job opportunities.

Gen Z Around the World, 109–118
Copyright © 2024 Alfe M. Solina, Tamather M. Shatnawi, Liane Vina G. Ocampo, Luisa M. Martinez and Ronalyn I. Garcia
Published under exclusive licence by Emerald Publishing Limited
doi:10.1108/978-1-83797-092-620241012

Professional Preparation During the Pandemic

Findings from the Global Gen Z Study highlight education as being one of their primary social concerns. Any impact on the quality of education can impact professional preparation for future career success. During the pandemic, 89% of countries worldwide implemented some form of nationwide school closures, affecting over 1.5 billion students globally (UNESCO, 2021). This had an especially significant impact on young people from disadvantaged backgrounds who may not have had access to critical technology or support to continue their education during school and university closures or remote operations.

In emerging countries, many Generation Z students struggled with a lack of access to technology and internet connectivity during the pandemic (World Economic Forum, 2022). Many reported difficulties keeping up with online classes and completing assignments (Nigam et al., 2021), and many schools lacked basic infrastructure such as electricity, water supply, and sanitation facilities. According to the Director of the UNESCO Institute for Statistics, these situations make it more challenging for students to continue their education during the pandemic (Montoya, 2020). In addition, many companies suspended their internship and apprenticeship programs, and others reduced their hiring, which has made it difficult for Gen Zers to gain valuable work experience while in school (PBS, 2020). It is not surprising then that a study by McKinsey found that 60% of European executives said they were struggling to find employees with the skills they need. Another study found that 70% of African youth lack the skills needed for the modern job market (ILO, 2018).

Unemployment

A study by the National Bureau of Economic Research in the United States revealed that job seekers during the pandemic faced an average of 13.6% more competition than before the pandemic. This led to a decline in employment opportunities for young workers, particularly those in the service sector (Federal Reserve Bank of St. Louis, 2020). In addition, many industries that typically employ younger workers, such as in hospitality and retail, experienced significant disruption. The Chartered Institute of Personnel and Development (CIPD) found that almost two-thirds of employers had canceled or deferred job offers to graduates due to the pandemic (CIPD, 2020) and recorded an unemployment rate of 11.6% among 16- to 24-year-olds in the 3 months prior to January 2021, compared to 4.4% for all age groups. This is the highest rate for this age group since 2016 (ONS, 2021). The Eurostat data also showed that the youth unemployment rate in the European Union was 17.3% in February 2021, up from 15.4% in February 2020. In Africa, the pandemic caused a decline in job opportunities, particularly in the informal sector, which was a major source of employment for young people (African Development Bank, 2020). Sixty-eight percent of African youth said they had been negatively affected by the pandemic, with 25% reported having lost their jobs. This has been the case in other developing countries as well as the unemployment rate among youth rose to nearly 28% (ILO, 2021). Starting their careers in this type of economic downturn left many Gen Zers furloughed or laid off, resulting in them struggling financially to catch up both professionally and financially.

Factors Impacting Professional Lives

Several factors impact Generation Z's professional lives. These include workplace flexibility, financial security, mental well-being, social interaction, and meaningful work.

Workplace Flexibility

While remote work became more prevalent during the pandemic and may have offered flexibility for many employees, it also created new challenges for Gen Zers. A study by Eurofound (2022) found that young people who were working remotely reported more difficulties in managing their workload and feeling isolated than older colleagues. Moreover, many young people began their careers working remotely during the pandemic, unlike those in older generations who had many years to establish interpersonal connections and embed themselves in the organizational culture in an in-person job. A survey by Prospects (2021) found that almost half of students and graduates in the United Kingdom found it difficult to work from home during the pandemic due to a lack of suitable workspace or distractions. While they may struggle long-term with remote work, perhaps more of a hybrid model where they can work from home part of the time and work onsite other times, would work well for them. But it may not be that they need a formal hybrid structure with specific days of the week designated for working remotely versus onsite but instead a fluid option that allows them, if possible, depending on the job role, to choose their day-to-day work location based on what would work best in any given time.

Financial Security

Of all the social concerns reported in the Global Gen Z Study, the most prominent concerns are related to financial security. These include education, poverty, the cost of higher education, the economy, access to viable and affordable housing, unemployment, and access to health care. In looking by region, though, some of these issues emerge at a higher rate in each region's top three rated social concerns as outlined in Table 12.1. Africa's rates were tied, so the top four are included.

It appears that access to health care is the most prominent issue followed by cost of higher education, access to viable and affordable housing, and poverty.

While all of these concerns focus on life affordability, one particularly interesting point centers on access to viable and affordable housing. The ability to access an accommodation can affect where one is able to work geographically for in-person jobs, and for those with remote jobs, if their housing is feasible for

Table 12.1. Top Issues Related to Employment by Region.

Region	Issue Related to Employment in the Region's Top Three Highest Rated Concerns
Africa[a]	Poverty
	Access to viable housing
	Cost of higher education
	Unemployment
African-Islamic	Poverty
	Access to health care
Catholic Europe	Access to viable and affordable housing
Confucian	None
English-Speaking	Cost of higher education
	Education
Latin America	Education
	Access to health care
	Poverty
Orthodox Europe	Access to health care
	Education
Protestant Europe	None
West and South Asia	Access to viable and affordable housing
	Cost of higher education

[a]Not included in the World Values Survey.

working from home. As the European Commission (2021) reported, nearly 40% of young people in Europe face difficulties in accessing adequate housing.

Asian countries also faced similar challenges. According to a report by the United Nations Economic and Social Commission for Asia and the Pacific (2020) housing affordability is a significant challenge for many young people in the region. As such, with remote work becoming more prevalent, many young people have been looking for larger apartments or houses to accommodate their work-from-home needs, further driving up housing costs. Furthermore, as many students have had to take their classes online during the pandemic, there has been a decrease in demand for student housing, causing landlords to switch to short-term rentals or increase prices for nonstudent tenants (BBC News, 2021). This trend has been particularly pronounced in places like New York City, Singapore, Tel Aviv, Zurich, and Hong Kong (Arky, 2023). Because of these factors, many Gen Zers from across the globe have opted to move home with their parents, live with roommates, spend more on housing than they can sustainably afford, or forgo their dreams to buy rather than rent (McKinsey &

Company, 2022). The pandemic exacerbated this problem, as many young people lost their jobs or experienced a reduction in their income, making it even harder for them to afford housing.

According to findings from the Global Gen Z study, as a result of the pandemic, 23% of Gen Zers looked for a new job, and 14% changed career paths. In looking at the two career-related behaviors by regions (World Values Survey Association, 2022), there are some differences highlighted in Table 12.2.

While there were some differences in rates for "looked for a new job" when comparing at a regional level, it is clear, many Gen Zers from across the globe sought out new job opportunities because of the pandemic. Some may have lost their jobs due to temporary layoffs, permanent business closures or position cuts, or scheduling scale-backs where the hours worked would not yield a sustainable income. Others, though, may have left on their own to find a new job that is more secure, safe, and/or higher income.

The rates by region for "changed career paths" also varied somewhat. However, it is clear that many in Generation Z, regardless of region, sought new career trajectories because of the pandemic. Some may have searched for recession-proof fields, higher income professions, or even just had a reckoning during the pandemic as to what was most important and thus, followed their passions. What is interesting, though, is that nearly all regions had higher rates of looking for a new career path over a new job, likely indicating that most have a desire to find a professional opportunity within their current industries to capitalize on their training and/or experience in their fields.

Mental Well-being at Work

The pandemic brought many issues to light, with one being the importance of mental well-being, particularly in the workplace. While this concern cuts across

Table 12.2. Career-Related Behaviors as a Result of the Pandemic.

Region	Looked for a New Job	Changed Career Paths
Africa[a]	25%	21%
African-Islamic	19%	14%
Catholic Europe	11%	16%
Confucian	5%	13%
English-Speaking	34%	11%
Latin America	33%	27%
Orthodox Europe	18%	9%
Protestant Europe	16%	14%
West and South Asia	35%	6%

[a]Not included in the World Values Survey.

all generations, it is pervasive with those in Generation Z. One Gen Zer in the Global Gen Z Study said an ideal career is one in which there is "no excessive mental strain (stress, depression, etc.)."

The National Association of Colleges and Employers (2020) reported that more than 70% of employers expressed that the pandemic had negatively impacted the mental health of their employees. And, Gen Zers shared a similar sentiment. For young people, the pandemic exacerbated mental health issues, increased suicidal ideation, and created challenges to their social and emotional wellbeing (U.S. Department of Education, 2021). However, these impacts were not isolated to those in the United States. In fact, young people worldwide were disproportionately affected by COVID in terms of their mental health (World Health Organization, 2022). A 2021 study by Young Minds found that 80% of young people felt that the pandemic had made their mental health worse, and were more likely to report a decline in mental health during the pandemic (Eurofound, 2022). Further, in 2021, more than 16,000 adolescents and young adults in Europe cited that their depression and anxiety symptoms were higher during the pandemic compared to their prepandemic state. Specifically, the study found that rates of depression symptoms increased from 14.9% prepandemic to 19.6% during the pandemic, and rates of anxiety symptoms increased from 20.6% before the pandemic to 27.6% during the pandemic (O'Connor et al., 2021).

Social Interaction at Work

The lack of social interaction, particularly during the pandemic, also created difficulties in preparing Gen Zers for and engaging them in the workforce. A Study by NORC (2021) found that 45% of those in Generation Z indicated that the pandemic made it more difficult to maintain friendships. In the workplace, Gen Zers are less engaged, with most not feeling connected to their coworkers (Gallup, 2022). But, lack of opportunity to connect due to the pandemic is not the only underlying force impacting Generation Z's interaction with others. Prior to the pandemic, Cigna (2018) found that Generation Z identified as the loneliest generation, with factors like feeling shy, being isolated and alone, and no one really knowing them as affecting their loneliness. As social interaction is critical to feeling like you are a part of a team, supporting social interactions will be important to engaging Gen Z in the workplace.

Meaningful Work

When asked what their ideal career would entail, overwhelmingly, the Gen Zers in the Global Gen Z Study highlighted the importance of engaging in meaningful work – a job and workplace that makes them happy, tasks that are fulfilling, and making a contribution that matters. One Gen Zer said, "I want to enjoy and be passionate about what I am doing. Income matters, but being passionate is my priority." While financial security is important, many indicated that as long as they had income to pay the bills, they would rather work in a job that fulfills them and make less money than in a job that is not fulfilling for higher pay. This sentiment also aligns with their motivation of feeling a sense of accomplishment and wanting to make a difference for others as indicated in the Global Gen Z Study.

Freelancing and Entrepreneurship

According to findings from the Global Gen Z Study, 43% of Gen Zers greatly identified as intellectual, and 29% as visionary, two key characteristics reflective of an innovative mindset. In addition, 58% greatly identified as curious, and 51% as determined, which may predict a forthcoming persistence in developing solutions to challenging problems as they age – well-aligned with engaging in freelancing and entrepreneurship.

Freelancing is the act of selling a product or service, full-time or part-time, without being employed by someone else and includes such work as graphic design and app development as well as grocery delivery and dog-walking. Many Gen Zers have a positive outlook on freelancing. In a study conducted by free-lancing platform, Fiverr, the majority of those in Generation Z believe that freelancing is "a smart option in an uncertain economy" (2023, para. 7) and that their desire to learn is a motivating factor for engaging in freelance work. Further, a study of US workers by Upwork (2022) found that 43% of Gen Zers engage in freelance work. While the percentage of freelancers was lower (20%) in the Global Gen Z Study, the participant pool included those who were full-time students with only part-time work during school as well as those not employed at all. When disaggregated by the older half of the generation (mid-late twenties), the rates are higher at 21%, whereas the younger half of the generation (upper teens to low-twenties) has a rate of 15%. In looking by region, freelancing rates range from 16% in English-speaking countries to 33% in Confucian countries. Despite the variance and the small representation of participants by some regions, it is clear: Gen Zers around the world are freelancing.

Entrepreneurship differs slightly in that it involves creating a business, often employing others. Only 6% of those in the Global Gen Z Study reported running their own businesses. However, 37% of those who did were actually younger than 18 when they launched, perhaps indicating a viable trajectory for young people to enter into their careers at an early age.

Conclusion

Gen Zers were not spared of the impact of pandemic since a considerable per-centage have been affected as evidenced by the global unemployment rate among youth. Securing a job and starting their careers made them struggle as they propelled themselves to survive professionally and financially. Hence, Gen Zers have had to balance the drive for financial security and gainful employment with their desire for meaningful work where they can feel less stressed, connected, fulfilled, and make a contribution that matters.

As Gen Zers prepare for and enter the workforce, those who mentor, educate, and supervise this cohort will need to provide them with ample opportunity to clarify their values in terms of a professional trajectory that would feel fulfilling and financially secure, develop their social interaction skills, aid them in mindfulness work to eradicate stress, and help them discover various ways through which they can make a difference.

References

African Development Bank. (2020). *COVID-19 and youth employment in Africa.* https://www.afdb.org/sites/default/files/documents/publications/afdb-covid-19-and-youth-employment-in-africa-english.pdf

Arky, J. (2023). 5 cities around the world with the priciest real estate. https://finance.yahoo.com/news/5-cities-around-world-priciest-130143482.html

BBC News. (2021). The pandemic has changed the student housing market. https://www.bbc.com/news/business-56352652

Chartered Institute of Personnel and Development. (2020). COVID-19 and graduate recruitment: What employers are doing. https://www.cipd.co.uk/Images/covid-19-graduate-recruitment-employers-doing_tcm18-86259.pdf

Cigna. (2018). *Cigna U.S. loneliness index.* https://www.multivu.com/players/English/8294451-cigna-us-loneliness-survey/docs/IndexReport_1524069371598-173525450.pdf

Deloitte. (2021). Global Millennial and Gen Z survey. https://www.deloitte.com/global/en/about/people/social-responsibility/millennialsurvey-2021.html

Eurofound. (2022). *Living, working and COVID-19.* https://www.eurofound.europa.eu/data/covid-19

European Commission. (2021). *Youth guarantee: Tackling youth unemployment and promoting inclusive youth entrepreneurship.* https://ec.europa.eu/social/main.jsp?catId=1161

Federal Reserve Bank of St. Louis. (2020). *COVID-19's impact on young workers.* https://www.stlouisfed.org/on-the-economy/2020/may/covid19-impact-young-workers

Fiverr. (2023). Globally, 67% of Gen Zers freelance or are planning to, over 1 in 5 cite dissatisfaction with working a full-time job as a motivator. https://www.businesswire.com/news/home/20230309005181/en/Globally-67-of-Gen-Zers-Freelance-or-are-Planning-To-Over-1-in-5-Cite-Dissatisfaction-with-Working-a-Full-Time-Job-as-a-Motivator

Gallup. (2022). Generation disconnected: Data on Gen Z in the workplace. https://www.gallup.com/workplace/404693/generation-disconnected-data-gen-workplace.aspx

International Labour Organization. (2018). *Future of work in Africa: Harnessing the potential of digital technologies for all.* https://www.ilo.org/wcmsp5/groups/public/—africa/—ro-abidjan/—sro-addis_ababa/documents/publication/wcms_618529.pdf

International Labor Organization. (2021). *The impact of the COVID-19 pandemic on jobs and incomes in G20 economies.* G20 Saudi Arabia. Organisation for Economic

Co-operation and Development. https://www.ilo.org/wcmsp5/groups/public/—dgreports/—cabinet/documents/publication/wcms_756331.pdf

McKinsey & Company. (2022). *Roommates, childhood bedrooms, and $226,000 on rent: Gen Z's housing future*. https://www.mckinsey.com/~/media/mckinsey/email/genz/2022/09/20/2022-09-20b.html

Montoya, S. (2020). *Rethinking school infrastructure during a global health crisis*. UNESCO Institute for Statistics. https://uis.unesco.org/en/blog/rethinking-school-infrastructure-during-global-health-crisis

National Association of Colleges and Employers. (2020). *Job outlook 2021*. https://www.naceweb.org/store/2020/job-outlook-2021/

Nigam, S., Chatterjee, K., & Biswas, T. (2021). Impact of the COVID-19 pandemic on the education sector in India. *Journal of Education and e-Learning Research, 8*(1), 1–10.

NORC. (2021). *Gen Z and the toll of the pandemic*. https://apnorc.org/projects/gen-z-and-the-toll-of-the-pandemic/

O'Connor, R. C., Wetherall, K., Cleare, S., McClelland, H., Melson, A. J., Niedzwiedz, C. L., O'Carroll, R. E., O'Connor, D. B., Platt, S., Scowcroft, E., Watson, B., Zortea, T., Ferguson, E., & Robb, K. A. (2021). Mental health and well-being during the COVID-19 pandemic: Longitudinal analyses of adults in the UK COVID-19 mental health & wellbeing study. *British Journal of Psychiatry, 218*(6), 326–333. https://doi.org/10.1192/bjp.2020.212.

Office for National Statistics. (2021). *Labour market overview, UK: March 2021*. https://www.ons.gov.uk/employmentandlabourmarket/peopleinwork/employmentandemployeetypes/bulletins/uklabourmarket/march2021

PBS. (2020). *Internships get canceled or go virtual because of pandemic*. https://www.pbs.org/newshour/nation/internships-get-canceled-or-go-virtual-because-of-pandemic

Prospects. (2021). *Graduate careers in a post-COVID world*. https://www.prospects.ac.uk/employer-insights/graduate-careers-in-a-post-covid-world

UNESCO. (2021). COVID-19 educational disruption and response. https://en.unesco.org/news/covid-19-educational-disruption-and-response

United Nations Economic and Social Commission for Asia and the Pacific. (2020). *Asia and the Pacific SDG progress report 2020*. https://www.unescap.org/resources/asia-and-pacific-sdg-progress-report-2020

Upwork. (2022). *Freelance forward 2022*. https://www.upwork.com/research/freelance-forward-2022?utm_source=PartnerCentric&utm_medium=affiliate&utm_campaign=10078_Skimbit%20Ltd.&irclickid=wvjz1OxVHxyNWC4XYXRgA0-fUkAVuh3vPwLLXk0&irgwc=1&

U.S. Department of Education. (2021). *Education in a pandemic: The disparate impacts of COVID-19 on America's students*. https://https://www2.ed.gov/about/offices/list/ocr/docs/20210608-impacts-of-covid19.pdf

World Economic Forum. (2021). What is 'the great resignation'? An expert explains. https://www.weforum.org/agenda/2021/11/what-is-the-great-resignation-and-what-can-we-learn-from-it/

World Economic Forum. (2022). *Coronavirus has exposed the digital divide like never before*. https://www.weforum.org/agenda/2020/04/coronavirus-covid-19-pandemic-digital-divide-internet-data-broadband-mobbile/

World Health Organization. (2022). *COVID-19 pandemic triggers 25% increase in prevalence of anxiety and depression worldwide.* https://https://www.who.int/news/item/02-03-2022-covid-19-pandemic-triggers-25-increase-in-prevalence-ofanxiety-and-depression-worldwide

World Values Survey Association. (2022). *World values survey.* https://www.worldvaluessurvey.org/WVSContents.jsp

Young Minds. (2021). *Coronavirus: Impact on young people with mental health needs.* https://youngminds.org.uk/media/4290/coronavirus-report_may-2021_final.pdf

Chapter 13

Societal Concerns

*Diana Bogueva[a], Dora Marinova[b], Natalia Waechter[c]
and İsmail Hakkı Tekiner[d]*

[a]University of Sydney, Australia
[b]Curtin University of Technology, Australia
[c]University of Graz, Austria
[d]Istanbul Sabahattin Zaim University, Turkey

Abstract

Generation Z is already an influential global cohort with strong stances about social, economic, and climate justice. According to the Global Gen Z Survey, worries about racism, sexism, limitations on personal freedom and homophobia are the top social justice concerns while education, poverty, access to health care, access to viable and affordable housing, and cost of higher education top the list of economic justice concerns. Added to the list of concerns is climate change, including its intragenerational and intergenerational impacts, and in the words of one participant, "none of the rest… matter if we don't have a planet to live on."

Keywords: Climate change; environment; social justice; discrimination; economic justice; climate justice

Generation Z has already emerged as an informed and influential global cohort. Individual role models and activists, such as Greta Thunberg campaigning for action against climate change, and Malala Yousafzai fighting for the human rights of women, are powerful global voices. There are similar role models in each country around the world.

Beyond individual activists, the global Generation Z cohort seems to be concerned about issues that impact society as a whole. At the core of societal concerns is the notion of justice or fairness in the way people are being treated (Collins, 2023) in and by society and include social justice, economic justice, and climate justice. Although social justice has a culturally complex nature conceptualized differently

Gen Z Around the World, 119–127
doi:10.1108/978-1-83797-092-620241013

throughout human history, it reflects the need and ability for everyone to participate on equal grounds in social and political life (Thrift & Sugarman, 2019). It is based on recognition of differences and different identities as well as the freedom of individuals to express their views. The concept of social justice is also a counterpoint to human propensity to act unfairly toward particular social groups or individuals, including exert power, discriminate, cause physical and psychologic harm, and restrict access to resources and opportunities (Bales, 2018). Economic justice is based on the concept that the economy is more successful if everybody has opportunities to thrive and achieve their full potential (Hayes, 2022). Climate change is a global phenomenon but the range of impacts varies according to geographic locations, with the socially weaker sections of society exposed to more severe consequences giving rise to concerns about climate justice (IPCC, 2022).

All justice categories have the interlinked dimensions of intragenerational and intergenerational justice, which is respectively, justice between people from Generation Z, and between people of Generation Z and other generations such as Baby Boomers, or Millennials. Although some government policies, for example, related to inclusion or social mobility, may have intergenerational impacts, the aims of social and economic justice are predominantly intragenerational. Climate justice, however, is distinctively intergenerational based on the scientific evidence that accumulation of greenhouse gases is causing the planet to warm up triggering extreme weather, rising sea-levels, and changing temperature patterns (IPCC, 2022). It is important to note these intersections of justice as it frames the issues that are present in the societal concerns of Generation Z.

Societal Concerns

Based on findings from the Global Gen Z Study, the 10 most prominent societal concerns for Generation Z (see Table 13.1) fall into the three categories of justice. Not all 30 topics given to the participants to rate were issues of justice. Thus, it appears that justice, in general, was an overarching concern.

The shares of those who were not concerned about the top 10 issues were relatively low, starting with rates as low as only six percent for education and poverty and only up to 16% for homophobia. Hence, the majority of Gen Zers are concerned about these issues. In addition, only a few issues outside of the top 10 attracted relatively low levels of concern, such as border security (25% were not concerned), gun rights (24% were not concerned), and national debt (21% were not concerned). The issue about border security may be preoccupying politicians with commentators seeing it as "a point of obsession of our times" (Longo, 2017, p. 2), making it appear that it is already being addressed. Levels of concern about gun rights vary among countries influenced by existing laws and regulations. For example, there is no legal right to gun ownership in Australia, which contrasts with the position of the United States. Less restrictive gun laws result in higher levels of violence (Everytown Research & Policy, 2023). In the Global Gen Z Survey, gun safety was a concern for 60% of the participants in the United States compared to 53% in the rest of the world and only 42% in Australia. In regard to national debt, although Gen Zers are aware of the challenges surrounding national debt, they are prioritizing other issues over this, resulting in relatively lower concern (Pransky, 2021).

Table 13.1. Top 10 Societal Concerns of Gen Z.

Category and Issue	Very Concerned and Concerned	Somewhat and Slightly Concerned	Not Concerned
Social Justice			
Racism	65%	26%	8%
Sexism	61%	28%	11%
Limitations on personal freedom	59%	33%	8%
Homophobia	55%	29%	16%
Economic Justice			
Education	64%	30%	6%
Poverty	63%	32%	6%
Access to health care	63%	29%	8%
Access to viable and affordable housing	62%	31%	7%
Cost of higher education	60%	32%	8%
Climate Justice			
Climate change	60%	31%	9%

In looking at societal concerns across the World Values regions (World Values Survey Association, 2022), there are some revealing insights outlined in Table 13.2. The issue that falls into the top three for the most regions is racism (four of nine regions), which is the most prominent social justice issue across the globe. Representing all economic justice issues, the following concerns were in the top three for three of nine regions: Poverty, access to viable housing, cost of higher education, education, and access to health care. Climate justice, reflected by the concern "climate change", was in the top three for the Confucian region and Protestant Europe.

In the top three for both Asian regions (Confucian and West and South Asia) was internet security, which did not appear for any other region. Sexism was in the top three for Catholic and Protestant Europe, but no other region of the world. Limitations on personal freedom was a top three concern for Confucian region and Orthodox Europe.

Social Justice

The issues of racism, sexism, and homophobia are among the most concerning societal issues for Generation Z. It appears that this demographic cohort is much more attuned to reacting against social injustice and protecting its own identity, respect, and equality as they aspire to create a better society (Svetaz et al., 2020).

Table 13.2. Top Three Societal Concerns for Each Region.

Region	Societal Issue and Percentage Concerned or Very Concerned
Africa[a]	Poverty (87%)
	Access to viable housing (87%)
	Cost of higher education (87%)
	Unemployment (87%)
African-Islamic	Racism (74%)
	Poverty (74%)
	Access to health care (72%)
Catholic Europe	Racism (70%)
	Access to viable and affordable housing (70%)
	Sexism (69%)
Confucian	Climate change (45%)
	Internet security (44%)
	Limitations on personal freedoms (43%)
English-speaking	Cost of higher education (69%)
	Education (67%)
	Racism (66%)
Latin America	Education (93%)
	Access to health care (88%)
	Poverty (85%)
Orthodox Europe	Access to health care (67%)
	Limitations on personal freedoms (66%)
	Education (66%)
Protestant Europe	Climate change (80%)
	Racism (75%)
	Sexism (70%)
West and South Asia	Access to viable and affordable housing (80%)
	Cost of higher education (76%)
	Internet security (61%)

[a]Not included in the World Values Survey.

Generation Z believes in the quest for better and more humane, fair, and honest treatment. Being aware and seeing what is happening in the world around them, the young people do not want to build self-protection, anger, or hostility, but instead want to generate an environment of sympathy and equality where differences are welcomed. One participant in the Global Gen Z Study wrote: "If everyone was kinder, we wouldn't have sexism, racism, wars, etc. We'd be able to come together and love one another and find a solution for issues like climate change. We can challenge each other's beliefs and show different perspectives, which helps unite us. If someone feels heard, they're more likely to be kind."

Personal freedom is likely an important factor in Generation Z's desire for social justice. Given Generation Z's unprecedented sensitivity toward social justice (Hayek, 2021), it is not surprising that Generation Z poses challenges to established institutions within society, such as religious and political systems that may appear to limit the personal freedom of individuals based on particular identities. For example, previous research describes the American Generation Z as typifying the post-Christian world (White, 2017) where many values associated with personal freedom and beliefs previously influenced by the church are now being redefined and re-interpreted.

Economic Justice

Creating opportunities for everyone within the economy is the essence of economic justice (Hayes, 2022). Education is a prerequisite for participation in the economy and is a major societal concern for Gen Zers. Their concerns center on both the quality of education and the cost of higher education.

In a hyperlinked world where information is readily available, this generation demands instant answers, a different interactive and hands-on educational approach, and learning requirements compared to previous generations (Chalk, 2022). Statistically, Generation Z will become the most educated human generation that has ever lived on this planet (Annie E. Casey Foundation, 2020). However, in some countries such as the United States and Australia, these young people are amassing student debts higher than those of previous generations (Bareham, 2023). This is manifested as a concern – one of the top 10 societal concerns is the cost of higher education (see Table 13.1) and may potentially impact education-related decisions.

Concerns around poverty mirror those related to education; however, while education indicates opportunities, poverty expresses apprehensions about a growing gap between the richest and the poor, financial and economic outlooks as well as job security (Perna, 2022). Possible reasons for worries about poverty are increased costs of living, earnings not keeping up with inflation, disappearance of the middle class, and globalization that enhances poverty worldwide (Gecsoyler, 2022). Ranked ninth on the list of societal concerns, access to viable and affordable housing is in line with previous evidence that the cost of living, including housing affordability and expenses, unemployment, and uncertainty about the future are already causing unease for Generation Z (Garnham, 2022).

Despite the health-care sector viewing the digitally native Generation Z as bringing a new set of expectations (Halton, 2020), this generation indisputably worries about health-care access. This is particularly evident in relation to people of color, minorities, or Indigenous populations, many of whom are often let down by the existing health-care systems (Centers for Disease Control and Prevention (CDC), 2022). Related to their strong sense for social justice, many of Generation Z are already experiencing issues of mental health, increased stress, anxiety, and depression (Annie E. Casey Foundation, 2021) contributing to their concerns about access to health care.

Lived experiences can further impact Generation Z's health and opportunities for a just participation in the economy. For example, in the United States, "Gen Z faces chronic stress from many factors including school shootings, student debt, joblessness and even politics" (Annie E. Casey Foundation, 2021, para. 4). In countries which are already experiencing the immediate effects of global warming, such as the Philippines, climate change anxiety becomes a contributing factor in triggering mental health problems (Reyes et al., 2021). The COVID-19 pandemic further fueled anxiety with the effect on young people being more pronounced (Garnham, 2022). These young people need a mentor who can provide them with guidelines for holistic health and wellness and a consumer-centric health-care experience (Halton, 2020). However, the affordability and accessibility of such services can become barriers driving down preventative measures and help-seeking for mental-health services (McKinsey & Company, 2022).

Climate Justice

Climate justice emerged from the environmental movement with a focus on "local impacts and experience, inequitable vulnerabilities, the importance of community voice, and demands for community sovereignty and functioning" (Schlosberg & Collins, 2014, p. 359). This was in response to overwhelming evidence that human-induced climate change is the biggest threat of our times, impacting the natural environment but also human communities across the globe (United Nations, 2022). Climate change is the biggest injustice imposed on the poorest countries and the weakest sections of society whose rights to a safe environment, along with clean air and water are being compromised. The global challenges related to climate change are further linked to nature's wide range of ecoservices. As Rouf and Wainwright explain, social inequality and economic vulnerability are replicated in environmental disasters as "individuals who are hardest hit by climate change are often already vulnerable and have the least resources" (2020, p. e131).

The essence of climate change, however, is very much intergenerational when it comes to Generation Z. These young people already understand the importance of protecting the environment and that responding to climate change is critical for the planet and their own future (World Economic Forum, 2022). One Gen Zer in the Global Gen Z Study wrote, in response to what concerns topped the list, "none of the rest... matter if we don't have a planet to live on."

While Gen Zers are engaging in efforts to save the planet, they also know that these problems have been accumulating through the activities (or lack thereof) of previous generations since industrialization, including those behaviors of their parents and grandparents. The intergenerational perspective on climate justice is broadly voiced. Concerns about climate change are part of the top 10 list in the Global Gen Z Survey. Sixty percent indicate being very concerned, which is higher than the results obtained by the 2022 Deloitte survey (Deloitte, 2022) where 24% of Generation Z indicated being deeply concerned about climate change. While the results differ, what is known is that young people are strongly concerned about the environment.

Members of Generation Z have been extremely active in calling politicians, industrialists, and other influencers for genuine action on climate change by holding climate strikes, boycotting unsustainable products or companies, and participating in active disruptions (e.g., the protests of Extinction Rebellion). While young people no longer focus on political parties, they are seeking to engage in the democratic processes through alternative means that deliver direct and fast outcomes (Carnegie, 2022).

Conclusion

From an intergenerational perspective, Generation Z believes that it has been betrayed by society and previous generations by being poorer, having to deal with depression and the prospects of runaway climate change (Gecsoyler, 2022), and hence raises strong concerns. With previous research showing that 70% of Generation Z is involved in a social or political cause (Cooper, 2021), it is not surprising to see these young people speaking up for social, economic, and climate justice. They believe that society will become better when action is taken to address inequality and opportunities are provided to everyone to thrive.

With the enthusiasm of youth, Generation Z needs to resolve the layers of social, environmental, and economic problems being inherited from previous generations. These tasks are complex. Educators, parents, and supervisors need to provide platforms and opportunities not only for Generation Z's voices to be heard but also for new creative and leadership skills to be developed. The long journey ahead starts with the strong manifestation that Generation Z cares about justice. These young people need to be encouraged and supported to clarify their concerns and find ways for addressing them.

References

Annie E. Casey Foundation. (2020). *Statistics snapshot: Generation Z and education.* https://www.aecf.org/blog/generation-z-and-education

Annie E. Casey Foundation. (2021). *Generation Z and mental health.* https://www.aecf.org/blog/generation-z-and-mental-health

Bales, S. (2018). *Social justice and library work: A guide to theory and practice.* Chandos Publishing.

Bareham, H. (2023). *Which generation has the most student loan debt?* https://www.bankrate.com/loans/student-loans/student-loan-debt-by-generation/

Carnegie, M. (2022). *Technology has given young people a louder voice than ever before. Gen Z are angry – and unafraid to speak up.* https://www.bbc.com/worklife/article/20220803-gen-z-how-young-people-are-changing-activism

Centers for Disease Control and Prevention (CDC). (2022). What is health equity? https://www.cdc.gov/nchhstp/healthequity/index.html

Chalk. (2022). *Teaching the next generation: How Gen Z learns.* https://www.chalk.com/resources/teaching-the-next-generation-how-gen-z-learns/

Collins. (2023). *Definition of "justice".* https://www.collinsdictionary.com/us/dictionary/english/justice

Cooper, J. (2021). *Unleashing the power of Gen Z.* https://www.edelman.com/insights/unleashing-power-gen-z

Deloitte. (2022). *The Deloitte global 2022 Gen Z and Millennial survey.* https://www.deloitte.com/global/en/issues/work/genzmillennialsurvey.html

Everytown Research & Policy. (2023). *Gun safety policies save lives.* https://everytownresearch.org/rankings/

Garnham, C. (2022). *The Gen Z mental health wave – What is causing the surge?* https://healthmatch.io/blog/the-gen-z-mental-health-wave-what-is-causing-the-surge

Gecsoyler, S. (2022). *Gen Z aren't 'intolerant': We're just poor, fed-up and want real change.* https://www.theguardian.com/commentisfree/2022/nov/04/gen-z-intolerant-poor-illiberal

Halton, R. (2020). *Industry voices—Generation Z is a game changer for healthcare.* https://www.fiercehealthcare.com/practices/industry-voices-generation-z-a-game-changer-for-healthcare

Hayek, A. (2021). *Generation We: The power and promise of Gen Z.* Lioncrest Publishing.

Hayes, A. (2022). *Economic justice.* https://www.investopedia.com/terms/e/economic-justice.asp

Intergovernmental Panel on Climate Change (IPCC). (2022). *Climate change 2022: Impacts, adaptation and vulnerability.* https://www.ipcc.ch/report/sixth-assessment-report-working-group-ii/

Longo, M. (2017). *The politics of borders: Sovereignty, security, and the citizen after 9/11.* Cambridge University Press.

McKinsey & Company. (2022). *Addressing the unprecedented behavioral-health challenges facing Generation Z.* https://www.mckinsey.com/industries/healthcare/our-insights/addressing-the-unprecedentedbehavioral-health-challenges-facing-generation-z

Perna, M. C. (2022). *Deloitte: Almost half of Gen Z workers live with financial anxiety every day.* https://www.forbes.com/sites/markcperna/2022/05/23/deloitte-almost-half-of-gen-z-workers-live-with-financial-anxiety-every-day/?sh=366738f07073

Pransky, N. (2021). *3 reasons young voters don't care about the national debt – And 1 reason they should.* https://www.lx.com/politics/3-reasons-young-voters-dont-care-about-the-national-debt-and-1-reason-they-should/44941/

Reyes, M. E. S., Carmen, B. P. B., Luminarias, M. E. P., Mangulabnan, S. A. N. B., & Ogunbode, C. A. (2021). An investigation into the relationship between climate change anxiety and mental health among Gen Z Filipinos. *Current Psychology.* https://doi.org/10.1007/s12144-021-02099-3

Rouf, K., & Wainwright, T. (2020). Linking health justice, social justice, and climate justice. *The Lancet Planetary Health, 4*(4), E131–E132. https://doi.org/10.1016/S2542-5196(20)30083-8

Schlosberg, D., & Collins, L. (2014). From environmental to climate justice: Climate change and the discourse of environmental justice. *WIREs Climate Change, 5*(3), 359–374. https://doi.org/10.1002/wcc.275

Svetaz, M. V., Coyne-Beasley, T., Trent, M., Wade, R., Ryan, M. H., Kelley, M., & Chulani, V. (2020). The traumatic impact of racism and discrimination on young people and how to talk about it. In K. R. Ginsburg & Z. B. R. McClain (Eds.), *Reaching teens: Strength-based, trauma-sensitive, resilience-building communication strategies rooted in positive youth development* (2nd ed., pp. 307–334). American Academy of Pediatrics.

Thrift, E., & Sugarman, J. (2019). What is social justice? Implications for psychology. *Journal of Theoretical & Philosophical Psychology*, *39*(1), 1–17. http://doi.org/10.1037/teo0000097

United Nations. (2022). *Climate change the greatest threat the world has ever faced, UN expert warns.* https://www.ohchr.org/en/press-releases/2022/10/climate-change-greatest-threat-world-has-ever-faced-un-expert-warns

White, J. E. (2017). *Meet Generation Z: Understanding and reaching the new post-Christian world.* Baker Books.

World Economic Forum. (2022). *How to help Gen Z turn climate anxiety into action.* https://www.weforum.org/agenda/2022/11/generation-z-climate-change/

World Values Survey Association. (2022). *World values survey.* https://www.worldvaluessurvey.org/WVSContents.jsp

Chapter 14

Civic Engagement and Social Change

Elena Botezat[a], Ioan Fotea[b], Daniela Crisan[c] and Silvia Fotea[b]

[a]University of Oradea, Romania
[b]Emanuel University of Oradea, Romania
[c]Data Scientist, Romania

Abstract

Generation Z has already begun to impact our world, particularly through their social change behaviors, personal characteristics, volunteering, and entrepreneurial endeavors. In particular, Gen Zers around the world like to stay informed of societal issues, share information with others about those issues, and engage in personal behaviors and/or lifestyle changes to address those issues.

Keywords: Civic engagement; impact; personal characteristics; volunteering; entrepreneurship; social change

The world that Generation Z inherits is one of exciting discoveries and innovations, enabled and propelled by the internet at light speed across continents and cultures (Seemiller & Grace, 2017). But it is also a world of geopolitical turmoil, remorse, and fear. Generation Z experienced the post-9/11 world as young children in which acts of terror became ubiquitous, the global financial crisis of 2007–2008 which wiped off financial security and more currently the global COVID-19 pandemic which confronted humanity with the fragility of life itself (McMaster, 2020; Pichler et al., 2021). Therefore, it is understandable that Generation Z is feeling tired of being resilient and wants support and genuine change (Deloitte Global, 2022). As Adler (2013) insightfully stated, "Only such persons who are... at home in the world can benefit both by the difficulties and by the advantages of life" (p. 39). How can Generation Z feel at home in the world they inherit? Is there a path forward for them to belong and identify with this world they live in? Perhaps, through civic engagement and social change, there is. Participating in the community can offer people a sense of belonging, clarified social identity, as well as meaning and fulfillment (Botezat et al., 2020; Jeong et al., 2020; Rochester et al., 2010).

Gen Z Around the World, 129–137
Copyright © 2024 Elena Botezat, Ioan Fotea, Daniela Crisan and Silvia Fotea
Published under exclusive licence by Emerald Publishing Limited
doi:10.1108/978-1-83797-092-620241014

But what exactly are Generation Z's perspectives when it comes to civic engagement and social change? Findings from the Global Gen Z Study reveal how this generation engages in social change and how their personalities, behaviors, and group roles come into play in their engagement. In all these inquiries, the significant insight that surfaces is that embedded in Generation Z's mindset is the desire to have the satisfaction of knowing their life has meaning and it benefits the world.

The more the educators, supervisors, and parents from around the world understand Generation Z pathways of engagement in community issues, the more they can play a role in fostering, embracing, and empowering Generation Z to make a difference in world for their cohort and for others.

Social Change Behaviors

Despite the uncertainty and worry brought about by the COVID-19 pandemic, Generation Z members are aware that they will not always be able to solve all the problems, but at the same time they do not underestimate the importance of their own contribution. So, how frequently have Generation Z members engaged in social change behaviors? Table 14.1 shows the percentages of Gen Zers from the Global Gen Z Study who indicated sometimes (monthly), often (weekly), or regularly (daily) engaging in specific social change behaviors.

Staying informed and sharing information with others regarding social issues they are concerned about are the most frequent social change behaviors Generation Z engages in, while changing a personal behavior/lifestyle and refraining from buying goods or services from companies that do not support (or oppose) social issues they are the next most frequent behavior. Among the behaviors with the least engagement are supporting a political campaign, raising money for a social issue, participating in advocacy events, and donating money to organizations that work to address social issues.

When disaggregated by regions from the World Values Survey (World Values Survey Association, 2022), the top three behaviors are consistent. These are exhibited in Table 14.2.

There is a great similarity in the three most prevalent social change behaviors across regions. And, other than the African-Islamic region and Africa, the ordering of these behaviors across the regions were the same. The nuance to note is the differentiation in rates; for example, Stay Informed ranged from as low as 47% in the African-Islamic region and as high as 89% in Catholic Europe and Protestant Europe. However, in terms of a global peer personality, one can assert that Gen Zers from around the world are most engaged by doing low-time, low-risk, individual behaviors where they can get current event updates, as well as share stories and links through their social media platforms and newsfeeds with the tap of a button. However, having vast amounts of information that is widely, instantly, and freely accessible has created inherent risks of receiving disinformation, misinformation, and fake news, which can deeply affect Gen Zers as avid social media consumers (Shu et al., 2020).

Table 14.1. Frequency of Social Change Behavior in the Past 12 Months.

Social Change Behavior	At Least Monthly
Stayed informed about social issues I care about	82%
Shared information with others about a social issue I am concerned about	72%
Changed a personal behavior or my lifestyle to address a social issue I am concerned about	63%
Refrained from buying goods or services from companies that don't support social issues or oppose social issues I am concerned about	49%
Participated in community service related to a social issue I am concerned about	35%
Participated in a social media campaign around a social issue I am concerned about	35%
Signed a petition to support a social issue I am concerned about	34%
Donated money to organization that works to address a social issue I am concerned about	27%
Participated in an advocacy event (protest, marches, etc.) on a social issue I am concerned about	22%
Raised money for a social issue I am concerned about	18%
Supported a political campaign (fundraising, lobbying, canvassing for a candidate)	17%

Gen Zers can also engage in their own personal lifestyle choices, such as recycling or eating vegetarian, as a way to make a difference. With these types of activities, they have agency over their choices, and ultimately, behaviors.

Personal Characteristics of Engaged Generation Z Members

There seems to be a strong association between individuals' engagement in a social change behavior and the personal characteristics of compassionate and being responsible. Engaging in social change behaviors is aligned with feeling in harmony with oneself and others (Agronick & Duncan, 1998), liken to the nature of compassion. Further, compassion, can be defined as a reaction to human pain (Dutton et al., 2006), involving a response, action, or behavior that alleviates the suffering. It is not surprising then that compassion is related to social justice work (LeBlanc et al., 2021), social entrepreneurship (Miller et al., 2012), and humanitarian work (Blackstone, 2009).

Table 14.2. Top Three Social Change Behaviors for Each Region.

Region	Top Three Social Change Behaviors
Africa[a]	Shared information (65%) Stayed informed (61%) Personal behavior/lifestyle change (61%)
African-Islamic	Stayed informed (47%) Personal behavior/lifestyle change (43%) Shared information (42%)
Catholic Europe	Stayed informed (89%) Shared information (75%) Personal behavior/lifestyle change (52%)
Confucian	Stayed informed (70%) Shared information (65%) Personal behavior/lifestyle change (56%)
English-speaking	Stayed informed (86%) Shared information (74%) Personal behavior/Lifestyle change (65%)
Latin America	Stayed informed (89%) Shared information (82%) Personal behavior/lifestyle change (72%)
Orthodox Europe	Stayed informed (69%) Shared information (68%) Personal behavior/lifestyle change (55%)
Protestant Europe	Stayed informed (89%) Shared information (73%) Personal behavior/lifestyle change (63%)
West and South Asia	Stayed informed (83%) Shared information (63%) Personal behavior/lifestyle change (55%)

[a]Not included in the World Values Survey.

Responsibility is also tied to social change. Phrases like social responsibility and corporate responsibility, for example, tie the notion of responsibility for doing good for communities. On an individual level, how responsible a person feels was also found in different studies as a promising predictor of that person's social change behavior (Kaiser & Shimoda, 1999; Silke et al., 2021).

Given the connection of compassion and responsibility with social change behavior, it makes sense that Gen Zers who identify more with being compassionate and those who identify more with being responsible tend to have higher

Table 14.3. Characteristics and Personal Behavior/Lifestyle Change.

	Greatly Describes Me	Somewhat Describes Me	Does Not Describe Me
Compassionate	67%	58%	49%
Responsible	64%	60%	58%

rates of changing their personal behaviors or making a lifestyle change to address a social issue they care about, as seen in Table 14.3 shows this differentiation.

Other positive associations between personal characteristics and changing a personal behavior or lifestyle to address a social issue of concern included being practical, authentic, sensible, loyal, thoughtful, adaptable, inclusive, open-minded, cooperative, and determined. One negatively associated personal characteristic included being conservative. Additionally, Gen Zers who stay informed and who share information with others about social issues they are interested in also rated themselves higher in terms of being curious, collaborative, and realistic.

Volunteering

During the year prior to the Global Gen Z Survey, 35% of Gen Zers reported participating, at least monthly, in community service, and 36%, at least monthly, in a social media campaign around a social issue of concern. However, the COVID-19 pandemic created few opportunities for engagement (Kragt & Holtrop, 2019; Pokhrel & Chhetri, 2021), meaning that during normal circumstances, their engagement rates may have been higher. Table 14.4 highlights the volunteer rates of Gen Zers during the past year, in which data was collected during the pandemic.

Volunteering can support social change by contributing to personal development, whereby individuals get a glimpse of new perspectives that could change their beliefs and behaviors once they have enhanced a deeper understanding of a social problem (Burgess & Durrant, 2019; Vannier et al., 2021). There are

Table 14.4. Volunteer Rates.

Volunteer Hours During the Past Year	Percentage of Participants
Zero (0) hours	43%
1–10 hours	30%
11–40 hours	15%
>40 hours	12%

different ways to engage in volunteering: being a volunteer from home, helping a charity of the forces that keep our communities safe, or an event. In return, volunteers can acquire new skills, gain valuable experience, participate in networking opportunities, meet others, and feel a sense of accomplishment.

Whatever the future holds, two things are clear. Firstly, volunteering is an important form of social engagement that can connect different stakeholders and improve communities. Secondly, volunteering engages the humanistic side of individuals, such as empathy and compassion (Agronick & Duncan, 1998; Dutton et al., 2006).

Social Entrepreneurship

While some Gen Zers may opt to contribute their time through volunteerism or change a personal lifestyle behavior, others are contributing to the greater good through their professional endeavors. As Table 14.5 shows, findings reveal that some Gen Zers are already engaged in entrepreneurial endeavors to address a social issue. This can be linked with individuals who perceive crises as critical opportunities and suitable situations for implementing new ideas (Brown & Rocha, 2020). Since COVID-19 also accelerated digital transformation, Gen Zers can apply their digital skills to put in action their entrepreneurial intentions (Botezat et al., 2022).

Despite the overall low numbers, this generation is engaging in entrepreneurship. With more training, resources, and opportunities ahead of them as they age, this entrepreneurial spirit and subsequent endeavors will likely continue to grow.

Group Roles and Social Entrepreneurship

It is telling, though, Gen Zers who engage in social entrepreneurship more often engage in group roles that are different from those who do not engage in social entrepreneurship. Table 14.6 showcases this comparison.

Table 14.5. Entrepreneurial Endeavors Among Gen Zers to Address a Social Issue.

Entrepreneurial Endeavor	Percentage of Participants
Started an organization (in the community, at school)	6%
Invented or designed a product or process	5%
Started a nonprofit	5%
Created a business (freelance or corporation)	4%

Table 14.6. Comparison of Gen Z Group Roles and Entrepreneurship.

Group Role	Nonsocial Entrepreneurs	Social Entrepreneurs
Leading	44%	55%
Doing	77%	72%
Relating	65%	68%
Thinking	76%	76%

For one, social entrepreneurs engage in leading roles, which involve taking initiative, more often than nonsocial entrepreneurs. On the other hand, those who do not engage in social entrepreneurship engage in doing roles, which involve executing work given to them, more often than social entrepreneurs. This distribution is not surprising in that entrepreneurship often takes leadership to launch an organization or to create or invent something. And, while entrepreneurs can get into the details of executing work, it makes sense that they would spend more time leading than nonentrepreneurs.

Conclusion

Investigating the relationship between Generation Z's characteristics, preferences, and behaviors and their engagement in social change has a threefold utility. First, it helps Gen Zers better understand themselves and to become aware of their own social change behavior. Second, it offers guidance when educators, parents, or supervisors are working with Generation Z in an effort to leverage their engagement. Finally, it broadens the wide public understanding about Generation Z and their approach to social change.

Understanding civic engagement and social change behaviors can help educators, parents, and supervisors. These trusted adults can encourage Gen Zers to seek engagement opportunities that interest them and align with their passions, encourage them to think beyond lower-effort individual actions and consider involving themselves in larger endeavors for social change, challenge them with tasks that require an increased level of skill and commitment, foster their entrepreneurial spirit by teaching them strategies for social entrepreneurship, and help Generation Z entrepreneurs utilize knowledge gained from running their business to employing strategies for social change.

While it's easy to become overwhelmed by the many social issues of the contemporary world, it is important to remember that Generation Z is already leading positive change to make a difference.

References

Adler, A. (2013). *The science of living (Psychology Revivals)*. Routledge. https://doi.org/10.4324/9780203386750

Agronick, G. S., & Duncan, L. E. (1998). Personality and social change: Individual differences, life path, and importance attributed to the women's movement. *Journal of Personality and Social Psychology, 74*, 1545–1555. https://doi.org/10.1037/0022-3514.74.6.1545

Blackstone, A. (2009). Doing good, being good, and the social construction of compassion. *Journal of Contemporary Ethnography, 38*(1), 85–116.

Botezat, E., Constăngioară, A., Dodescu, A.-O., & Pop-Cohuţ, I.-C. (2022). How stable are students' entrepreneurial intentions in the COVID-19 pandemic context? *Sustainability, 14*(9). Article 9. https://doi.org/10.3390/su14095690

Botezat, E., Fotea, S. L., Marici, M., & Fotea, I. S. (2020). Fostering the mediating role of the feeling of belonging to an organization among Romanian members of Generation Z. *Studia Universitatis "Vasile Goldiş" Arad – Economics Series, 30*(4), 69–91. https://doi.org/10.2478/sues-2020-0025

Brown, R., & Rocha, A. (2020). Entrepreneurial uncertainty during the Covid-19 crisis: Mapping the temporal dynamics of entrepreneurial finance. *Journal of Business Venturing Insights, 14*, e00174. https://doi.org/10.1016/j.jbvi.2020.e00174

Burgess, G., & Durrant, D. (2019). Reciprocity in the co-production of public services: The role of volunteering through community time exchange? *Social Policy and Society: A Journal of the Social Policy Association, 18*(2), 171–186. https://doi.org/10.1017/S1474746418000076

Deloitte Global. (2022). *The Deloitte Global 2022 Gen Z & Millennial survey* (Annual 11th ed., p. 40). https://www2.deloitte.com/content/dam/Deloitte/at/Documents/human-capital/at-gen-z-millennial-survey-2022.pdf

Dutton, J. E., Worline, M. C., Frost, P. J., & Lilius, J. (2006). Explaining compassion organizing. *Administrative Science Quarterly, 51*(1), 59–96. https://doi.org/10.2189/asqu.51.1.59

Jeong, S., Bailey, J. M., Lee, J., & McLean, G. N. (2020). "It's not about me, it's about us:" A narrative inquiry on living life as a social entrepreneur. *Social Enterprise Journal, 16*(3), 263–280. https://doi.org/10.1108/SEJ-05-2019-0030

Kaiser, F. G., & Shimoda, T. A. (1999). Responsibility as a predictor of ecological behaviour. *Journal of Environmental Psychology, 19*(3), 243–253. https://doi.org/10.1006/jevp.1998.9123

Kragt, D., & Holtrop, D. (2019). Volunteering research in Australia: A narrative review. *Australian Journal of Psychology, 71*(4), 342–360. https://doi.org/10.1111/ajpy.12251

LeBlanc, L. A., Gingles, D., & Byers, E. (2021). Compassion: The role of compassion in social justice efforts. In J. A. Sadovoy & M. L. Zube (Eds.), *A scientific framework for compassion and social justice* (pp. 60–65). Routledge.

McMaster, G. (2020, January 28). *Millennials and Gen Z are more anxious than previous generations: Here's why [Education Research]*. University of Alberta. https://www.ualberta.ca/folio/2020/01/millennials-and-gen-z-are-more-anxious-than-previous-generations-heres-why.html

Miller, T. L., Grimes, M. G., McMullen, J. S., & Vogus, T. J. (2012). Venturing for others with heart and head: How compassion encourages social entrepreneurship. *Academy of Management Review, 37*(4), 616–640.

Pichler, S., Kohli, C., & Granitz, N. (2021). DITTO for Gen Z: A framework for leveraging the uniqueness of the new generation. *Business Horizons, 64*(5), 599–610.

Pokhrel, S., & Chhetri, R. (2021). A literature review on impact of COVID-19 pandemic on teaching and learning. *Higher Education for the Future, 8*(1), 133–141. https://doi.org/10.1177/2347631120983481

Rochester, C., Paine, A. E., Howlett, S., & Zimmeck, M. (2010). *Volunteering and society in the 21st century.* Palgrave Macmillan.

Seemiller, C., & Grace, M. (2017). Generation Z: Educating and engaging the next generation of students. *About Campus, 22*(3), 21–26. https://doi.org/10.1002/abc.21293

Shu, K., Wang, S., Lee, D., & Liu, H. (Eds.). (2020). *Disinformation, misinformation, and fake news in social media: Emerging research challenges and opportunities.* Springer International Publishing. https://doi.org/10.1007/978-3-030-42699-6

Silke, C., Brady, B., Boylan, C., & Dolan, P. (2021). Empathy, social responsibility, and civic behavior among Irish adolescents: A socio-contextual approach. *The Journal of Early Adolescence, 41*(7), 996–1019. https://doi.org/10.1177/0272431620977658

Vannier, C., Mulligan, H., Wilkinson, A., Elder, S., Malik, A., Morrish, D., Campbell, M., Kingham, S., & Epton, M. (2021). Strengthening community connection and personal well-being through volunteering in New Zealand. *Health and Social Care in the Community, 29*(6), 1971–1979. https://doi.org/10.1111/hsc.13340

World Values Survey Association. (2022). *World values survey.* https://www.worldvaluessurvey.org/WVSContents.jsp

Chapter 15

Leaving a Legacy

Corey Seemiller[a] and Meghan Grace[b]

[a]Wright State University, USA
[b]Plaid, LLC, USA

Abstract

Regardless of nationality, culture, or region of the world, one thing is true – Generation Z wants to make a difference. They are motivated by impacting others, want careers that have purpose and meaning, and find solace in shared values and interpersonal connections. Overwhelmingly, they believe that their ability to be loving, kind, respectful, and inclusive can create a more unified and connected world. They also believe that if they work together to find common ground as well as educate themselves and others, their generation can take individual actions and develop innovative solutions to address monumental world problems.

Keywords: Legacy; social change; innovation; collaboration; common ground; individual actions

Each generation leaves an imprint on society, whether through key inventions, transformative policies, cultural shifts, or the influence of inspirational people. And while it is still early in the lifespan of Generation Z, signs already point to significant contributions this generation is making and will make in the future. Regardless of nationality, culture, or region of the world, one thing is true – Generation Z wants to make a difference (Martin, 2022; Seemiller & Grace, 2019). They are motivated by impacting others; they want careers that have purpose and meaning; and, they find solace in shared values and connection through their relationships. They not only want to change the world; they are actually doing it. So, what does their world look like in the future? And, how will they go about working toward that world?

Gen Z Around the World, 139–145
Copyright © 2024 Corey Seemiller and Meghan Grace
Published under exclusive licence by Emerald Publishing Limited
doi:10.1108/978-1-83797-092-620241015

Issues They Will Leave Their Mark On

Given their wide range of social concerns, it isn't surprising that Gen Zers see their legacy as having improved, or further, having eradicated these concerns. When asked about how their generation will make the world a better place, open-ended responses were solicited from participants in the Global Gen Z Study. While they described many ideas, two themes emerged most frequently – they wanted to tackle issues related to the environment and social justice.

Saving the Planet

In terms of the environment, suggestions for their contributions ranged from engaging in personal lifestyle choices like recycling, not eating meat, and eliminating the use of plastic to larger structural changes like the reduction of the use of fossil fuels and holding corporations accountable for environmental impacts. One Gen Zer notes, "We will be the generation that drastically reduced greenhouse gasses and fossil fuel consumption."

While engaging in behaviors that contribute toward saving the planet can be motivated by economic reasons (i.e., saving money on electricity by keeping lights off) (Parzanko et al., 2021), many also believe that doing so is their primary legacy due to the severity of the situation. "By ending climate change, literally it is one of my only concerns regarding the future, I don't think ya'll understand just how dire the situation is. Like, I don't plan to have kids because of climate change, and I know a lot of others who think the same way," said one Gen Zer. Particularly in regard to their concerns about the environment, Gen Zers shared a similar sentiment – other generations are not taking these issues seriously and they certainly are not doing enough.

Social Justice

Diversity and social justice are also paramount for this generation (Pichler et al., 2021; Seemiller & Grace, 2019). As one Gen Zer reported, this generation will "find ways to be more inclusive and equitable," which is a sentiment shared by many. Another Gen Zer said, "I think that my generation is relatively more accepting than other generations, and I know a lot of people my age are realizing that the way we were taught things as kids aren't exactly how it has to be. I hope that enough people in my generation understand how deep prejudices run in American culture and the intersectionality of discrimination that people experience. With that understanding, we could teach a whole new generation what we had to learn ourselves."

Further, many have the desire to advocate for others to be their authentic selves, standing up to bigoted behavior. One said, "By sticking up for people's rights to live their life how they want to live it and allow people to be their true selves without having to worry about judgment from strangers." Some also believe their impact is more than just about changing hearts and minds; it is also about changing policies and laws that enhance diversity, equity, and inclusion.

"Get rid of old, biased, bigoted laws and norms for good," one Gen Zer reported. Overall, those in Generation Z see their legacy as not just a calling to save the planet and create an inclusive and just world but as their responsibility in making the world a better place.

How Does Generation Z Plan to Leave a Legacy?

Generations throughout history have left their legacies in many ways, including through cures for diseases, technological advancements, and contributions to world peace. Like those in previous generations, Generation Z is already thinking about the legacy they plan to leave in years to come. They are confident in being able to address unresolved issues that challenged older generations; they are ready to confront contemporary problems that have recently arisen and feel prepared to take on difficult situations that will come about in the future. Findings from the Global Gen Z Study point to six actions Gen Zers plan to take in their lifetimes to make the world a better place.

Love and Kindness

Of all the ways they plan to make the world a better place, overwhelmingly, being loving and kind was the most discussed among study participants. Gen Zers believe that their ability to be loving, kind, respectful, and inclusive can create a more unified and connected world, one in which everyone can, as one Gen Zer said, "lead with love." On the contrary, many believe that divisiveness, exclusion, oppression, and disrespect can lead to a fractured society, where real problems go unaddressed. One participant noted that Generation Z will change the world "by loving those around us. A lot of the issues we see in the world today stem from hate, but if we would love each other how we love our closest friends, then we would see all of these social issues melt away." While these notions might be liken to common colloquial saying, "love conquers all," when referring to the naivete of youth, this generation has a far-reaching voice through the power of social media and technology and the inherent desire to make a difference, putting them in the ideal position to spread love to others.

Other Gen Zers believe that love is a feeling exuded toward everyone and everything. One person explained this as, "My generation can make the world a better place by showing more love. And I'm not just talking about 'love' like caring about others, but I'm also talking about giving more love to our oceans, our forests, our beautiful planet, our people (we are ALL human), EVERY-THING needs some love right about now, and my generation and I need to give that love to each other to make our home a better place." This view demonstrates the complex interconnectivity of Generation Z's world in which love means more than an exchange between people but instead more of guiding approach to everyone and everything on the planet.

Working Together to Find Common Ground

When people only interact with ideas and people who are in perfect alignment with their values and opinions, they can experience confirmation bias (Britannica, 2022). Limiting information only to a certain set of ideals prevents the exploration of other viewpoints, which could be critical in solving a challenging issue. However, this generation values working together to solve society's issues. Many believe that being open-minded, asking questions, compromising, and listening can help them find solutions to monumental world problems. One participated noted, "Taking the time to listen to different sides to learn and understand not just to respond" is essential for making a difference. But, social media and news sites are filled with both contradicting information deemed to be factual and subsequent narratives critiquing the other side's apparent misinformation. Gen Zers' desires to listen and find common ground are up against this deeply-embedded cultural tension. Perhaps those in Generation Z will not only listen, compromise, and work together, but they will also find a way to break the information divisiveness cycle.

Being able to listen and dialogue for understanding can also help in accepting that there may be more than one right answer. This idea is summed up with one Gen Zer's words, "Just because you're 'right', that doesn't make me 'wrong'." Being open-minded can help in finding an optimal solution to a problem, which may be a conglomeration of many individual ideas, as well as validate others in their perspectives. Further, being able to effectively listen to and work with others with different perspectives can also foster thriving relationships built on respect, rather than cultivate disconnection or discord. "I think the idea that what we believe is true while everyone else is false is so wrong. We have so much to learn from others and we are not perfect or better than anyone else," said one Gen Zer. Many in this generation want to find solutions to real problems and build productive relationships, and they know that working together is critical for doing so.

Influencing Others

Gen Zers have been referred to as the "superhero generation" as they take to the streets to save humanity (Luttrell & McGrath, 2021). It's not surprising then that they like to be front and center engaging in dialogue, activism, and advocacy. Whether marching in a protest, boycotting products or companies, or canvassing for politicians, Gen Zers know that their actions have a collective influence on others' beliefs and worldviews. One Gen Zer noted, "Using the technology we have at our disposal to reach others" can allow them to share ideas, experiences, stories, and calls to action in just moments. Another added, "[We can make the world a better place] by the power of social media. Constantly sharing information around the world, [drawing] the attention different communities need." This generation has more tools at their disposal for influencing the masses than any other generation. It is likely they will continue to use their voice and their platforms to advocate for what they believe in.

Gen Zers also believe that by educating others about the impact of their daily actions, people may learn new perspectives and possibly change their behaviors. By "raising awareness…and teaching the next generations," said one participant, Gen Zers can model a better world for all. Another added, "Understanding that even small battles over words (semantics – slave vs enslaved person) can reshape the way people think." While it may be off-putting for older individuals to be educated by Gen Zers about inclusive language or day-to-day actions that can make an impact, many young people will likely not shy away from doing so as they see the repercussions of keeping quiet as having detrimental effects on the issues they care about.

Learning

With so much information at our fingertips through computers and smartphones, Generation Z is experiencing a type of information overload different from other generations when they were young adults (Vilchik et al., 2020). Despite possibly feeling overwhelmed, many appreciate their ability to DIY their own learning, whether getting information online, from others, or through more formalized educational outlets. But, they believe that any one source shouldn't be relied on to form an opinion and that it is important not to "believe whatever you read on the internet or media without doing your own research," said one Gen Zer. Another noted, "Be open minded, don't assume your solution is the perfect solution and everyone should agree with you. Actually look into issues and not just rely on social media or major news platforms to get your ideas and formulate opinions." While some might not know how to discern legitimate information, they are aware that the internet, social media, and even their social circles, in particular, offer "facts" that lack credibility.

Many also understand that they have to unpack or "unlearn," as many Gen Zers wrote, a lot of what they have already learned in order to relearn accurate information and confront "systemic oppression." In addition, they want to learn beyond the borders set for them, like "what hasn't been taught in history books and has been hidden by others," "problems that have been normalized for a long time," and "what's going on outside of their circle." It may end up being that if content feels off-limits to them, in terms of book bans and re-engineered school curriculum, this generation may seek out missing content on their own.

Individual Actions

A number of those in Generation Z also embrace the notion that one person can make a difference and that there is a value to "doing things within our reach," as one participant said. The collection of all their individual actions, such as being grateful, serving as a role model, and making small lifestyle changes to support causes they care about can ultimately create a better world for all. "I feel like our generation is very involved and [we] are constantly making changes to our mindset, behaviors, lifestyles, and bettering our communities," one participant said.

In addition, many Gen Zers believe that their commitment to serving their communities will make a far-reaching difference, whether that is through formal service or just helping others. "[Our generation is going to change the world] by investing more time into selfless endeavors we are passionate about – community service without obligation," a Gen Zer said. And given that 57% engaged in at least some volunteer work during the year prior to the study, which was during the pandemic, it is likely their commitment to their communities will continue into the future.

Solving Problems With Innovative Solutions

Many Gen Zers are ready to tackle big problems with creative solutions and believe that they must shift their focus to address issues that have been plaguing society. They intend to, as one said, "challenge the outdated beliefs of many of our parents/grandparents and strive to make it better than how they'll leave it." Some have resentment for older generations where one describes as "practically lighting the house on fire and then closing the door behind them," leading them to have to what another put as, "correct what the people ahead of us didn't" and further, fix what they broke in the first place.

For some Gen Zers, solving society's problems includes using solutions that are already in existence. One suggested "not focus[ing] on the capitalist practice of creating new technologies to tackle every problem – perhaps look to indigenous ways of thinking, farming." For others, it means, what one Gen Zer described as "fixing what is broken and replacing what can't be fixed." And for what can't be fixed, this generation is apt to start over and build a new way of life through reflection, dismantling, and rebuilding. One Gen Zer discussed the importance of "looking at the mistakes of the past and realizing that the system is so broken we might as well start from scratch." Another offered the idea of "simply working hard to dismantle structures that negatively affect the wellbeing of most people and replacing them with structures and systems that work well for everyone affected by them." This is a generation ready to deconstruct and reconstruct society's institutions to make them more effective, sustainable, and inclusive.

Conclusion

Since this study was conducted, we have seen war, technological shifts, a wavering economy, fundamental changes in laws and political leadership, disease, and social movements to address issues that were not even on the horizon when this study was conducted. With the world changing each minute of every day, it will be the deep understanding of the peer personality of Generation Z on both a global and local level that will help us all better grasp the capacities, hopes, dreams, and desires of a generation poised to take the reins and make a difference as the world continues to change and evolve.

References

Britannica. (2022). *Confirmation bias*. https://www.britannica.com/science/confirmation-bias

Luttrell, R., & McGrath, K. (2021). *Gen Z: The superhero generation*. Rowman & Littlefield.

Martin, C. (2022). *The rise of trusted influence: 3 key Gen Z trends to act on*. Edelman. https://www.edelman.com/insights/rise-trusted-influence-3-key-gen-z-trends-act

Parzanko, A. J., Balinska, A., & Sleczko, A. (2021). Pro-environmental behaviors of Generation Z in the context of the concept of homo socio-oeconomicus. *Energies*, *14*(6), 1597. https://doi.org/10.3390/en14061597

Pichler, S., Kohli, C., & Granitz, N. (2021). DITTO for Gen Z: A framework for leveraging the uniqueness of the new generation. *Business Horizons*, *64*, 599–610.

Seemiller, C., & Grace, M. (2019). *Generation Z: A century in the Making*. Routledge.

Vilchik, M. K., Egorchenkova, N. B., & Korobova, O. V. (2020). Information overload as one of the aspects of modern society. In N. L. Shamne, S. Cindori, E. Y. Malushko, O. Larouk, & V. G. Lizunkov (Eds.), *Individual and society in the modern geopolitical environment. European proceedings of social and behavioural sciences* (Vol. 99, pp. 942–949). European Publisher. https://doi.org/10.15405/epsbs.2020.12.04.108

Chapter 16

The Global Peer Personality of Generation Z

Corey Seemiller[a] and Meghan Grace[b]

[a]Wright State University, USA
[b]Plaid, LLC, USA

Abstract

This chapter offers a summary of the highlights from each chapter, culminating in the construction of the global peer personality profile of Generation Z. Characteristics, motivations, interpersonal connections, learning and communication preferences, values and concerns, career aspirations, and social impact are discussed.

Keywords: Peer personality; generations; global; make a difference; generation Z; generational cohort

Between globalization, the proliferation of the internet and social media, along with shared experiences like economic recessions and the pandemic, it is not surprising that Gen Zers from around the world share elements of a universal peer personality.

Who is the Generation Z Global Cohort?

Like every generational cohort, Generation Z has a nuanced peer personality. Their characteristics, motivations, and worldviews have been shaped by those around them and by the forces and events surrounding their upbringing.

Open Hearted With a Sense of Commitment

Overall, this is a generation that sees themselves as loyal, responsible, thoughtful, compassionate, and open-minded. They care about others and the world around them and want to work in collaboration to address our challenging problems.

Gen Z Around the World, 147–152
Copyright © 2024 Corey Seemiller and Meghan Grace
Published under exclusive licence by Emerald Publishing Limited
doi:10.1108/978-1-83797-092-620241016

Intrinsically Motivated to Achieve and Impact Others

Overwhelmingly, Gen Zers are motivated intrinsically, wanting to do something because of an internal drive to do so. They are motivated by feeling accomplished, whether that is witnessing their efforts come to fruition, advancing up the ladder, or simply learning something new for self-improvement, all forms of personal growth motivators. They are also motivated by impacting others, which are positive relations motivators. For example, being able to advocate for causes they care about and not let others down are paramount for them.

More Realistic Than Optimistic

Gen Zers tend to be more realistic than optimistic, although 74% indicate being slightly or generally optimistic about their futures and 72% believe good things will happen for them. The range is only 65%–81%, indicating that regionally, optimism levels are fairly static. While they have some confidence in their own futures, they tend to not look as favorably on others. Only 50% slightly or wholly believe that people are inherently good. Given the many events that have occurred in the short lifetimes of those in Generation Z, it is not surprising that they are more grounded and realistic. However, they are not without hope and are likely the most optimistic when they can be a part of the solution that makes a positive impact.

What is Important in Their Connections With Others?

Gen Zers tend to highly value relationships, especially those where a deeper and more meaningful connection can be built. They are eager to offer their support, dedication, and loyalty to those they care about and those they work with.

Shared Values

In both friendships and romantic relationships, having shared values is more important than any other factor, including affiliation with a group or organization, shared culture, close proximity, similar hobbies, and physical appearance. It isn't surprising then that parents, who they likely share values with, are the number one influencer across all regions; they serve as their primary advice-givers about many topics, but often also about money. Many think highly of their parents as nearly half are motivated by pleasing or impressing them. So, their guidance can certainly result in Gen Zers sharing values with their parents.

Gen Zers are also influenced by siblings and friends, with those groups also being a part of their inner circles. It's not surprising then that those outside of their inner circles, like celebrities, social media influencers, and politicians, are generally the least influential. Given their trust in those closest to them, it makes sense that they would be motivated by wanting to make a difference for them as well.

Working With, but Not Leading Others

Overall, the majority of Gen Zers from every region like working in groups. Those who like working in groups tend to be more optimistic. Perhaps increasing group work could spur a more optimistic outlook in Gen Zers or perhaps optimistic Gen Zers see the good in others they work with. Gen Zers most often engage in group roles that reflect Doing and Thinking versus Relating and Leading. Because of this, Gen Zers may more readily join a group but then prefer opportunities to roll up their sleeves and get to work rather than engaging in agenda-setting and teambuilding.

How Do They Learn and Communicate?

Gen Zers like to give and receive information in ways that are personalized, whether that is through learning by applying new information in a context that makes sense for them, communicating in person in a way that aligns with their preferences and styles, or sharing personalized photos and videos on social media.

Watching and Practicing Are Foundational to Learning

Gen Zers believe the most effective learning modalities are experiential and demonstrated. They want to watch others do something and then try it themselves. What they find most enjoyable, however, is different and includes social and interpersonal, which involves learning with and around others. Further, likely stemming from changes in learning modalities during COVID-19, what they engage in is not what they find most effective or enjoyable. Those modalities include intrapersonal and video-based.

In an effort to appeal to their preferences, it is important for those teaching or training Gen Zers to diversify and possibly scaffold their pedagogies. For one, having them watch and practice might be a good first start for learning, followed by having them employ what they learned with or around others. While independent learning modalities were readily used by those in Generation Z, it is likely that their overuse during the pandemic triggered a high level of self-reported engagement with lower levels of enjoyment and effectiveness. However, these modalities can be flexible, innovative, and productive despite their utility perhaps not being as evident to those in Generation Z. Thus, it may be helpful to weave those modalities among other ways of instruction, like integrating a short video or worksheet into a hands-on or group learning experience.

Face-to-Face Communication is Key

Of all communication modalities, Gen Zers prefer face-to-face. While this may be reactionary to the inordinate amount of virtual communication that occurred during the pandemic, studies prior to the pandemic also found face-to-face the preferred method of communication (Seemiller & Grace, 2019). While some Gen

Zers might be the first to pick up their phones and send a message, they do actually crave human connection.

Social Media Provides Varied Spaces for Specific Purposes

When they are online, though, they gravitate toward certain platforms for specific purposes. They use Instagram for sharing expertise, influencing, and following others, whereas they use WhatsApp for sharing information about themselves and YouTube for learning. All three modalities have the ability to incorporate visual imagery such as photos or videos as a way to communicate. These images can help bring material to life.

What is Important to Them?

Overall, most Gen Zers simply want to live a life of meaning and purpose, where they can impact the issues they care about most and engage in work that offers financial security and for some, an opportunity to work for themselves.

Financial Security

A vast number of Gen Zers want to live their lives free from worrying about money. They want to work in a job that pays a living wage that would ensure they are financially secure and are already saving for a rainy day, given that nearly a quarter of any discretionary income they had would end up in a savings account. While they believe it is important to have financial security, they don't want to work in jobs they don't like just for the paycheck. And, they don't want to squander all of their extra funds and miss out on purchasing nongrocery food and beverage items and consumer goods, which bring enjoyment to their lives. They are reluctant to invest and aren't quick to donate or give their money away to family and friends.

In terms of money management, this generation leans toward those they know to get advice – for instance, their parents. Some seek out information online, while very few actually get advice or resources from people who have credentials or backgrounds in financial management.

Their attitude is telling. Gen Zers want to work in a job they enjoy in order to make the money they need and to live the good life they want. It will be likely that this mission will continue to drive them into specific careers and to make life choices that support this outcome.

Fulfillment

Gen Zers want a life filled with meaningful experiences, ones that make a difference for others. In particular, they crave careers where they are able to see their impact every single day. And, as long as they have financial security in terms of their income, many would choose meaning over money for their careers.

In addition to meaning, many also want to ensure they have support and resources to maintain mental well-being as well as opportunities for social interaction with friends and family, in and out of the workplace.

Entrepreneurship and Sustainable Career Fields

Gen Zers are generally innovative and entrepreneurial, harboring a mindset of being intellectual, visionary, determined, and curious. It's not surprising then that the members of Generation Z from all world regions engage in freelancing as either a full-time or part-time job, with older ones freelancing at higher rates than younger ones. Some may be doing it as a side hustle to supplement their income, whereas others are doing so for their full-time work. As freelancing will continue to grow around the world, it will be likely that Gen Zers take the lead, both for financial reasons and flexibility and balance reasons.

While many are still young or just entering their career fields, it makes sense that not quite as many have started their own businesses, perhaps with employees and/or a storefront, as have freelanced independently. But, for 37% who had launched a business endeavor, they did so before the age of 18. As the Generation Z cohort ages, it may be likely that more will engage in entrepreneurship, particularly as they will be better armed with financial resources, skills, credentials, and networks.

For those in traditional workplaces, the pandemic appeared to have impacted their occupational choices. Many changed jobs, either because they were forced out of their roles with layoffs or they opted for a new path. Some also entirely changed career fields, perhaps realizing that some jobs are safer and/or more recession-proof than others or simply because the pandemic served as a values-clarifying force for many, leading them to possibly question their choice in career trajectory.

Social, Economic, and Climate Justice

It's not unusual for young people to have many concerns about the way society functions, especially if it is done so by elders who can be blamed for the world's woes. Gen Zers are universally concerned with issues that reflect social justice (racism, sexism, homophobia, limitations on personal freedom), economic justice (education, poverty, healthcare, housing, cost of higher education), and climate justice (climate change). The number one issue globally and for most regions was racism.

There were some geographic nuances related to social concerns. For example, economic concerns were highest among regions with higher levels of poverty, access to affordable and accessible healthcare was higher in regions that did not have socialized healthcare, internet security was most prominent in Asian regions, and gun safety was more of a concern in the United States, specifically.

Impacting the World Through Individual Action

Gen Zers generally engage in social change behavior at the individual level. They stay informed about issues, share information about causes they care about, adjust their personal behavior or lifestyle to align with an issue they care about, and refrain from buying goods or services from companies that don't support their personal values. They also readily participate in community service and engage in social media campaigns. They aren't as likely to raise or donate money for a cause.

The two biggest issues they focus their energy on include those related to the environment and those related to social justice. They believe that if they express love and kindness to one another, work together to find common ground, influence others, learn new information, take individual action when they can, and solve problems with innovative solutions, that they can change the world.

Conclusion

With each passing day, new events and new situations influence generational cohorts. Wars, recessions, political movements, natural disasters, and inventions can all impact the worldviews, preferences, and behaviors of a generation. While these impacts will undoubtedly leave their marks, the peer personality of Generation Z, developed over the course of their adolescence and young adulthood, will likely stay somewhat intact. As they age, this peer personality may show up differently given their life stage; however, this is a generation that will likely see themselves as loyal, innovative, and caring, with a desire to make the world a more fair, just, and sustainable place.

Reference

Seemiller, C., & Grace, M. (2019). *Generation Z: A century in the making*. Routledge.

Index

Printed and bound by CPI Group (UK) Ltd, Croydon, CR0 4YY

11/04/2024

14482405-0003